the

A Step-by-Step Guide to SPSS for Sport and Exercise Studies

Statistical Package for the Social Sciences is the most widely used statistical software for data analysis in sport and exercise science departments around the world. This book is the first guide to SPSS that employs examples directly from the field of sport and exercise.

Using a variety of screenshots, figures and tables, this book demonstrates how students can open data files from different programmes, transform existing variables, compute new variables, split or merge data files, and select specific cases, as well as how to create and edit a variety of different tables and charts. The book uses clear step-by-step demonstrations to show how students can carry out and report a number of statistical tests.

Offering a comprehensive guide to SPSS functions, the book also explains the unavoidable jargon that comes with some statistical tests, and gives examples of how different statistical tests can be incorporated in sport and exercise studies. This book will be of great interest to any student wanting to learn about the features of SPSS.

Nikos Ntoumanis is Senior Lecturer in Sport and Exercise Psychology, Leeds Metropolitan University.

A Step-by-Step Guide to SPSS for Sport and Exercise Studies

Nikos Ntoumanis

ROUTLEDGE
Taylor & Francis Group

London and New York

First published 2001
by Routledge
2 Park Square, Milton Park, Abingdon, Oxon, OX14 4RN

Simultaneously published in the USA and Canada
by Routledge Inc.
270 Madison Ave, New York NY 10016

Routledge is an imprint of the Taylor & Francis Group

Transferred to Digital Printing 2006

© 2001 Nikos Ntoumanis

Typeset in Times by MHL Typesetting Ltd, Coventry, Warwickshire

British Library Cataloguing in Publication Data
A catalogue record for this book is available from the British Library

Library of Congress Cataloging in Publication Data
A catalog record for this book has been requested

ISBN 0-415-24978-3

Printed and bound by CPI Antony Rowe, Eastbourne

This book is dedicated to my family for their continuous support and encouragement throughout my life.

Contents

Preface

This book intends to fill in a clear gap in the literature. Although SPSS is the main computer software used for statistical analysis in most sport and exercise science departments, there are no available SPSS guides with sport- and exercise-specific examples. Therefore, sport and exercise students have to resort to SPSS guides which use examples from business, economics, sociology, or other social sciences. However, in the author's experience, students often have difficulties relating these examples (e.g., relationship between smoke concentrations in urban cities and rates of depression) to their area of research. This is especially a problem when they have to select and perform appropriate statistical tests for their dissertations and poster presentations. This book attempts to address this problem by using examples from sport and exercise science only. It is intended for students enrolled in sport and exercise degrees who have only a basic understanding of statistics. It should be pointed out that this guide provides a demonstration of the main options and statistical analyses of SPSS and should not be considered as a comprehensive SPSS guide.

A further problem with existing SPSS guides is that they do not give a detailed description of how students can perform various tests or rearrange their data. To address this problem, this guide includes step-by-step demonstrations of a sequence of different dialog boxes (screenshots). Another problem that is often observed is that students are puzzled with the large amount of information in the output of different statistical tests. This book offers them appropriate advice which focuses their attention on the parts of the output which are the most important and appropriate to their basic level of statistical understanding.

The book describes each SPSS menu separately. In each menu, most of the options are explained and examples are given. The book is organised in five chapters. Chapter 1 presents a brief introduction of SPSS. Chapter 2 explains how data can be organised and rearranged to facilitate statistical analysis. Chapter 3 presents a number of statistical tests which are commonly employed in sport and exercise science. Chapter 4 shows how SPSS can produce and modify a wide variety of charts and tables. Lastly, Chapter 5 presents miscellaneous options, such as how to obtain more information about the variables of a data file or how to run scripts. More detailed information about the statistical tests described here (e.g., their assumptions or the mathematical formulae that underlie them) can be found in the statistical texts listed in the Suggested Reading section at the end of this book.

This guide describes SPSS version 10. Versions 7 and higher were to a very large extent similar to version 10, so this guide will probably be useful with future versions. Please note that in this book, statistical symbols (e.g., r, F, p), SPSS menus and options have been *italicised*. Furthermore, while UK spelling has been used throughout the book, the SPSS options have retained their original US spelling.

Acknowledgements

The comments and suggestions of the following colleagues are gratefully acknowledged: Dr Costas Karageorghis, Professor Alan Nevill, Professor Stuart Biddle, and Dr Jean Whitehead. Of course, any flaws or mistakes in the book should be attributed entirely to me. I also appreciate the comments of some of my students on earlier drafts of this book. I would like to thank the staff at Routledge for helping make this book possible, especially Edwina Welham, Simon Whitmore, and Mark Majurey. Furthermore, I would like to acknowledge the kind permission of SPSS® Inc. to use their screen images. Finally, I am indebted to my family and a few selected friends, for their continuous encouragement and emotional support throughout this project.

1 Introduction

In the area of sport and exercise students and researchers often face important questions. For example, in sport psychology, a student may be interested in examining whether the pre-competitive anxiety levels of a group of athletes can be predicted by a number of psychological variables. In exercise physiology, another student may want to examine the degree to which a particular training programme has improved the aerobic capacity of a group of runners. In biomechanics, one may be interested to look at differences in the take-off velocity in the long jump between elite and non-elite athletes. In motor control and learning, a student may find it exciting to investigate whether the number of errors in a complex motor skill will vary between high and low anxiety conditions. In the area of exercise promotion, a student may want to test the hypothesis that frequency and duration of exercise will relate to body fat percentage.

To answer these and many more questions, a student needs to be familiar with certain statistical tests. Some of these tests (e.g., t tests, chi-square, correlation analysis) can be performed by hand, but most of the others (e.g., MANOVA, factor analysis) are too complicated and would require a significant amount of time and statistical knowledge. Even some of the simpler tests can be exceptionally time consuming when the sample size of a data set is large. Fortunately, with the advent of modern computers most statistical tests can be performed within a few seconds. However, first of all, one needs to know how to enter a data set into a computer file. Furthermore, one must be familiar with the environment of the statistical software because it is not very difficult to select an inappropriate option, or omit an important option, and obtain inappropriate results. Even when the procedure is correct, one needs to be able to understand and use the most important parts of an output. Furthermore, it is important for a student to be able to present the results in a dissertation or a poster in a technically appropriate manner. In addition, a student may want to create tables and charts which will illustrate the results of statistical tests. Lastly, a student should be in a position to rearrange and reorganise a data file, for example, to separate males and females, or to rank athletes according to their strength levels.

SPSS (Statistical Package for the Social Sciences) can meet these requirements. SPSS is a comprehensive statistical programme with a wide variety of options and statistical analyses available for social scientists. It includes a number of statistical tests which can be used to describe data and examine various research hypotheses. Some of these tests are very common in the literature (e.g., *t* tests, correlation analysis), whereas others are employed less often (e.g., discriminant analysis). With SPSS you can create and edit a wide variety of tables and figures (charts) which describe and summarise one or more variables. Although there are many statistical programmes available in the market, SPSS is the most preferred choice of Sport and Exercise Science departments around the world. This is because SPSS offers a wide variety of options and it is a user-friendly programme (honestly!).

The structure of this book is based on the presentation of four main SPSS windows: Data Editor, Output, Syntax, and Chart Editor. For an explanation of these windows, see *New* in the *File* menu. The Chart Editor is available only when you double-click and activate a chart. Each window has a number of menus; within each menu there are various options. The most popular of these options are represented in a toolbar at the top of the window. The Data Editor window (Figure 1) has the following menus: *File, Edit, View, Data, Transform, Analyze, Graphs, Utilities, Window,* and *Help*.

The Output window (Figure 2) has two unique menus, *Insert,* and *Format,* but it does not have the *Data* and *Transform* menus.

The Syntax window (Figure 3) has one unique menu, *Run,* but it does not have the *Data, Transform,* and *Insert* menus.

Lastly, the SPSS Chart Editor (Figure 4) has four unique menus: *Gallery, Chart, Series,* and *Format*. However, it does not have the *Data, Transform, Insert, Utilities* and *Window* menus.

When you first open SPSS, you are presented with a small window (Dialog box 1) which includes a number of options. You can *Run the tutorial* if you are a new SPSS user or if you have questions that are not covered in this book! If you just want to enter new data select *Type in data* (see *Data Entry* below). The next two options (*Run an existing query* or *Create new query*) will open a data file which is saved in another application (software). To retrieve this data file, the system

Figure 1

Figure 2

Figure 3

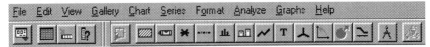

Figure 4

administrator of your university should provide you with a username and a password. Lastly, you can open an already saved SPSS file by selecting *Open an existing data source* or *Open another type of file*. If you do not want this dialog box to appear every time you open SPSS, tick *Don't show this dialog in the future*.

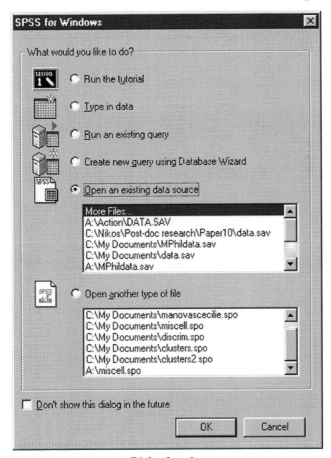

Dialog box 1

Data Entry

Each row in a data file should represent a different study participant and each column should correspond to a different measure (e.g., date of birth, gender, type of activity, enjoyment of main sport, etc.) of a particular participant. Therefore, you should enter new data horizontally until all measures of the first participant have been inserted. Then you can go to the second row and enter the data for the second participant, etc.

It is very important that you label all variables and give details about their format. Click the *Variable View* tab at the bottom of Figure 5. *Variable View* is not available in SPSS 9 or in any earlier versions (use the *Define Variable* option in the *Data* menu instead). In *Variable View*, ten different columns appear which provide information regarding the characteristics of each variable in the data file.

Note that, whereas in the *Data View* variables are represented in columns, in *Variable View* variables are represented in rows. In the *Name* column you can give a short name to a new variable in the data file. Note that the name of a variable should be normally no more than eight characters long. In the *Type* column you can specify the type of a variable. Click on a cell and a new button will appear ⋯. Click on this button and you will be presented with Dialog box 2. Select the *String* option if a variable is nominal (i.e., if it has letters instead of numbers, such as the names of sport clubs). Also, select this option if you want

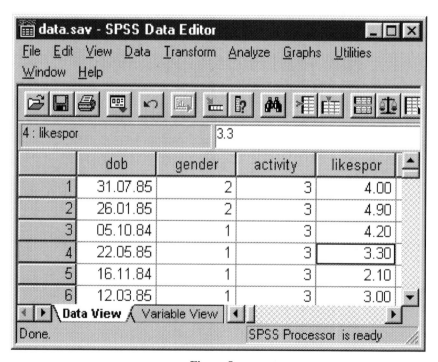

Figure 5

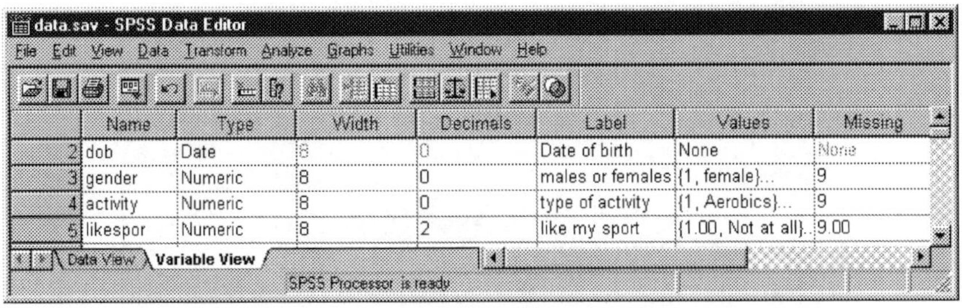

Figure 6

to name a variable with a combination of numbers and letters. By default, you can use up to eight characters to name the values of a string variable, but you can alter this restriction here. Select the *Numeric* option if a variable consists of numbers only. Select the *Date* option if the values of a variable consist of dates (e.g., date of an experiment, or date of birth of athletes).

The third column in Figure 6 is called *Width*. Click on a cell and use the arrows to modify the width of a variable. The fourth column, *Decimals*, lets you specify the number of decimals to use for each numeric variable. With the fifth column, *Labels*, you can give a more detailed description of a variable because you are not restricted to eight characters.

You can use the sixth column, *Values*, to label the values of a variable. Click on a cell to activate the button ![...]. In Dialog box 3, the variable *activity* describes the main sport of a sample of pupils. Each sport (value) has been given a code and a description (e.g., code 1 for Aerobics). After you label the first sport, click on *Add* and carry on in the same way with the second sport. When you finish the labelling of all sports, click *OK*. If you want to view the labels of values instead of their numeric codes (e.g., if you want to view Aerobics instead of 1) in the data file, select the *Value Labels* option in the *View* menu.

The seventh column in Figure 6 is called *Missing*. If the data have missing values you should specify them in Dialog box 4. For example, if a variable has values ranging from 1–5, you can use the number 9 as a code to indicate missing values. Depending on the range of scores, you may need to use different codes

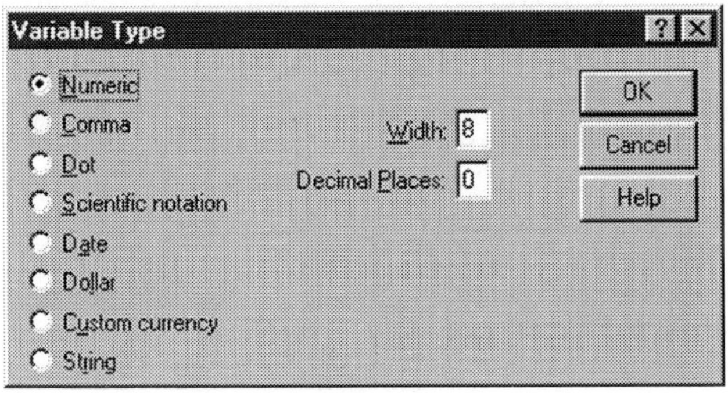

Dialog box 2

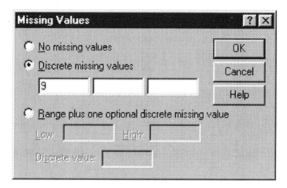

Dialog box 3

Dialog box 4

for the missing values of different variables. For example, you cannot use 9 to indicate missing values of a variable that has a range of possible scores from 1 to 100.

The next two columns in Figure 6, *Columns* and *Align*, let you specify the width of a column and the alignment (*left*, *right*, or *center*) of the values in the column. The last column, *Measure*, is used to identify the level at which a variable is measured. There are three levels. The first, *scale*, represents numeric variables (see *Type* above) measured on an interval or ratio scale. An interval scale has equal intervals of measurement, but there is no absolute zero (e.g., performance scores of divers or gymnasts). In contrast, a ratio scale has equal intervals as well as an absolute zero (e.g., measurements of time or height). The second *level* is *ordinal*, and refers to a ranking of variables, but with no indication of how much better one variable is compared to another (e.g., high, medium, and low dribbling skill). The third *level* is *nominal*, and describes participants in distinct groups (e.g., males and females). The *ordinal* and *nominal levels* should preferably have a combination of letters and numbers (e.g., 1 = males, 2 = females; see *Values* above). For a detailed explanation of the different *levels*, see Vincent (1999).

2   Data handling

File

New

SPSS has a variety of different types of files. The most frequently used ones are: the Data file (*.sav) which stores the data, the Output file (*spo), which stores charts, tables, and results of statistical analyses, and the Syntax file (*sps) which experienced SPSS users can use to run SPSS commands.

Open

With this option you can open a data file, an output file, or a syntax file. The data files can originate from SPSS (*.sav), or from other programmes such as Systat, Lotus, and Microsoft Excel.

To open an Excel data file, you must specify at the bottom of the dialog box that you want *Excel (*.xls)* files to be displayed only (Dialog box 5). Then, locate the folder where the Excel file is stored, highlight the file, and click *Open*.

A new dialog box (Dialog box 6) will appear which will ask you to select the parts of the Excel file you want to import.

The first row of the Excel file should contain the names of the variables. Tick the option *Read variable names from the first row of data* to label the imported variables (columns) in SPSS with the variable names that appear in the first row of the Excel file. Excel has multiple *worksheets* and you can specify which worksheet you want to open. If you want to open a part of a worksheet, you can specify a *range* of cells to be imported. In Dialog box 6, SPSS will import the first twenty rows (*1–20*) from the first two columns (*A* and *B*).

Note that if you have SPSS version 9 or an earlier version, and you want to open an Excel data file, you need first to save that file as Excel version 4. To find out which version of SPSS you have, select *About* in the *Help* menu.

Read Text Data

Use this option to open ASCII or text data files. These are very basic types of data files and are often used as a 'common currency' to exchange data files

Dialog box 5

Dialog box 6

between different software. Data files from software not supported by SPSS (e.g., Statistica) have to be saved as text files in the original software, so that SPSS will be able to read them. Similarly, if you want to open your SPSS data file (*.sav) in another software which does not support SPSS, you must save the SPSS data file as a text file (see *Save As* below).

First locate in your computer the appropriate text data file. Then click *open* in Dialog box 7.

A text wizard appears with six steps. At step 1 (Dialog box 8), SPSS asks you whether the *text file matches a predefined format*. Select *Yes* if you have used the text wizard before to create a data format (see step 6 below). If you have not

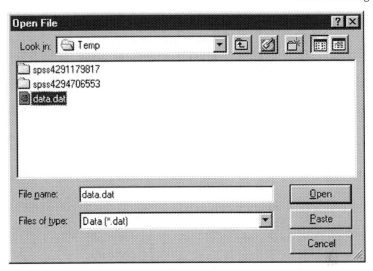

Dialog box 7

used the text wizard before, select *No*. At the bottom of the text wizard you can
see a preview of the data file. Click *Next >*.

At step 2 (Dialog box 9), you need to specify how the variables are arranged
in the original data file so that SPSS will know where the values of one variable
begin and where they finish. The different variables can be separated (*delimited*)
in the original file by a specific character such as a comma, a space, or a tab. In
such a case, the variables have the same order (variable 1 followed by variable 2,
etc.) for all cases (participants), but they are not necessarily in the same column
location (e.g., variable 1 of case 2 may not be located straight under variable 1 of
case 1). When each variable is recorded in the same column location for each
case you need to use the *Fixed width* option. With this option no delimiters are
required and the variables are arranged one after the other without spaces
between them.

At step 2, you should also specify whether the original data file has *variable
names at the top of the file* or not. At the bottom of the text wizard you can see a
preview of the data file.

At step 3 (Dialog box 10), identify on *which line number the first case begins*.
If the first line contains the variable names, then you should type 2 (i.e., the first
line begins on line 2). At this step you also need to specify how many lines
represent a case (participant). You are strongly advised to use only one line per
case. You can choose to import *all cases*, a certain number of cases (*the first n
cases*), or *a percentage of the cases*.

At step 4 (Dialog box 11), the text wizard shows a preview of how vertical
lines separate the variables in the original data file. If the separation is not
correct, you can move a vertical line to the correct position (*modify*), *insert* a

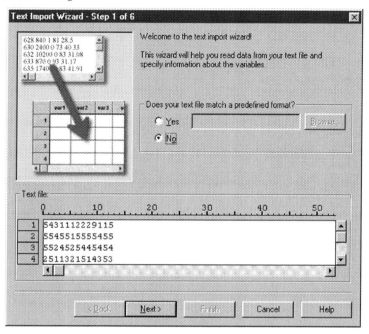

Dialog box 8

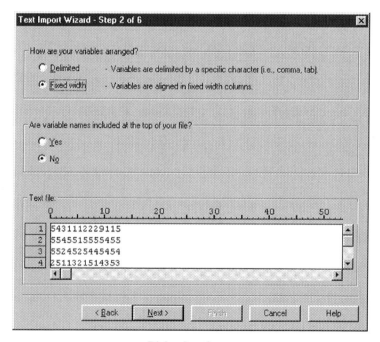

Dialog box 9

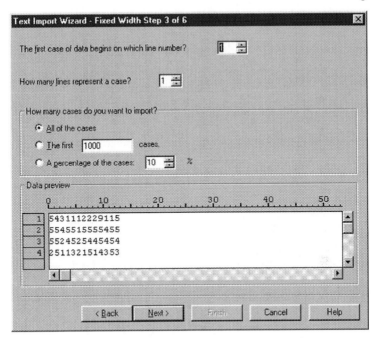

Dialog box 10

new vertical line, or *delete* an existing one. In Dialog box 11 there are 13 variables separated by 13 vertical lines.

If at step 2 (Dialog box 9) you had specified that the *variables should be delimited by a specific character*, then step 4 would have had a different dialog box (Dialog box 12). At the top of the text wizard you would have needed to specify *which delimiter appears between variables* (e.g., *space*). Also, the data preview would have been different with each variable appearing in a different column.

Let us continue from Dialog box 11. At the next step, step 5 (Dialog box 13), highlight one variable at a time in the *Data preview* window and specify its *name* and type (*data format*). The variable name should contain no more than eight characters. No spaces are permitted between the letters. If you have specified at step 2 (Dialog box 9) that *variable names are included at the top of the file*, then these names would have appeared in the *data preview* of *Dialog box* 13. For the different types of *data formats* see *Data Entry* in Chapter 1. Click *Next >*.

At the last step, step 6 (Dialog box 14), you are given the chance to *save this file format for future use*. Select *Yes* if you have other similar text files and you want to import them in a similar way. If you select *Yes*, next time you open a new similar text file you can indicate that the new *file matches a predefined format* (see step 1, Dialog box 8).

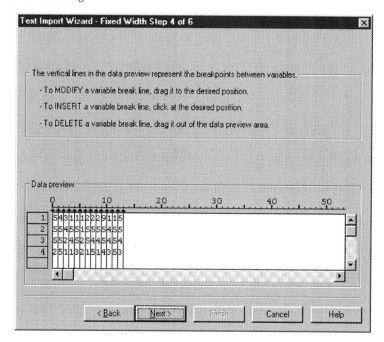

Dialog box 11

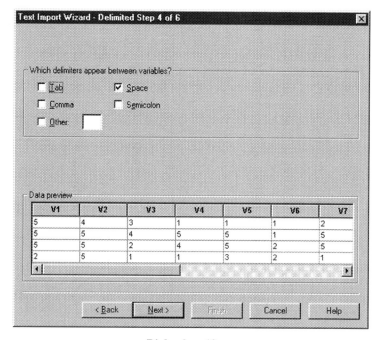

Dialog box 12

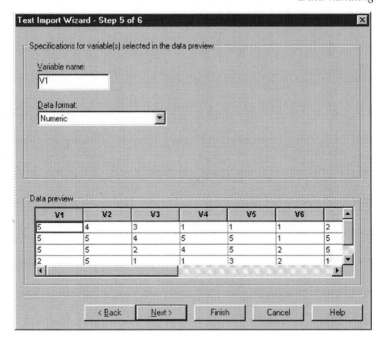

Dialog box 13

If you are an experienced SPSS user, you may want to paste the commands onto the *Syntax* window. Otherwise, select *No*. Click *Finish*, and the text data file will be imported into SPSS. Save the new file as a SPSS data file (*.sav).

Save As

Data files can be saved as earlier SPSS data file versions, as Excel files, or as text files (ASCII).

Display Data Info

This option provides useful information regarding a data file, the variables it contains, their labels and their format. It is similar to the *File info* option in the *Utilities* menu, but it is used to display information for stored files only, and not for a file which is open. Table 1 is an example of using this option.

Apply Data Dictionary

This option is useful when you are working with a new data file which has some variables in common with an existing data file. To save you the trouble of applying labels, missing values, and formats to these variables (see *Data entry* in

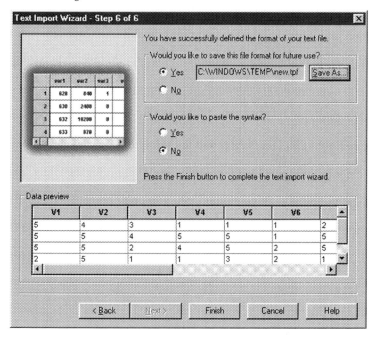

Dialog box 14

Table 1

```
SYSFILE INFO:c:\data.sav
File Type:     SPSS Data File
Creation Date:
Creation Time:
Label:      Not Available
N of Cases: 0
Total # of Defined Variable Elements: 129
# of Named Variables: 129
Data Are Not Weighted
Data Are Uncompressed
File Contains Case Data
Variable Information:
Name            GENDER    * No label *            Position 3

     Measurement level: Nominal
     Format: F8.2  Column Width: 8  Alignment: Right
    Missing Values: 9.00
     Value    Label
      1.00     female
      2.00     male
```

Chapter 1), locate the existing data file using *apply data dictionary*, and click *OK*. SPSS will apply for you the labels, missing values, and formats to these common variables based on the information stored in the existing file. Variables that are not common in both files are not affected. Also, the common variables do not have to be in the same order in the two files. Note that if the variable type is not the same in both files (e.g., if variable A in the new file is *string* and in the existing data file is *numeric*) only the variable label is applied.

Page Setup

This option is available in an Output window only. In the first dialog box, similar to a Microsoft Word document, you can specify the *size*, the *orientation*, and the *margins* of the output page (Dialog box 15). Click on the *Printer* button to change the printer or its properties.

Click *Options*. In the *Header/Footer* tab you can provide a title for the header and the footer (Dialog box 16).

Click on the *A* button in the middle of the dialog box to change the font size, type, and colour of the title. The next three buttons change the justification of the text. Click on the next four items if you want to print the date, time, page

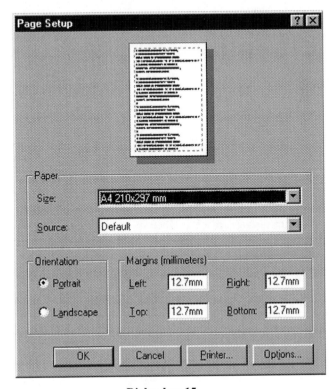

Dialog box 15

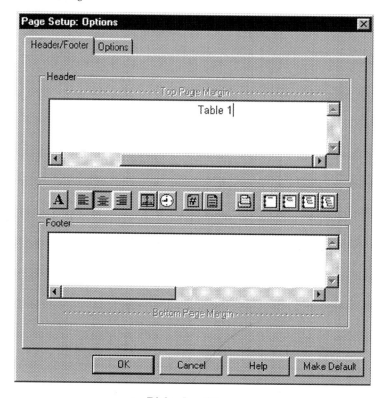

Dialog box 16

number, and the name of the file. Click on the last four icons if you want to change the level of the title heading (see *Outline* in the *Edit* menu).

Click on the *Options* tab in Dialog box 16. Under *Printed Chart Size* you can specify the size of the printed chart relative to the page. The chart can be left *as it is*, or it can reach *full page, half page,* or *quarter page height.* The chart's width-to-height ratio is not affected by these changes. Note that the maximum increase in a chart's size is reached when its outside frame (see *outer frame* in the *Chart* menu) reaches the left and right borders of the page.

Lastly, in Dialog box 17, you can increase or decrease the distance between printed items (tables, charts, and texts), and change the pagination of the printed pages.

Print Preview

This option is available in an Output window only. As in Microsoft Word, you can use *print preview* to view pages before they are printed.

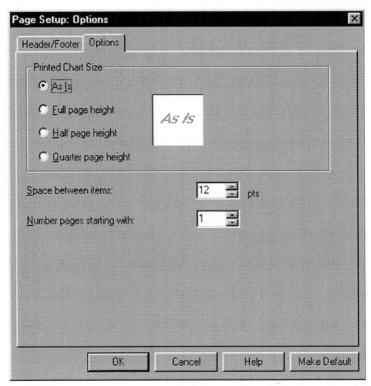

Dialog box 17

Print

You can print *all visible output* or a whole data file. Alternatively, you can *select* and print certain parts of an output or a data file. To print a section of a data file, you need to highlight it first. To select parts of an output, click with the mouse on the corresponding headings on the left-hand side of the output. To select multiple consecutive parts press Shift on the keyboard, and while pressing, click on the appropriate headings. To select multiple non-consecutive parts press Control on the keyboard, and while pressing, click on the appropriate headings. To remove a heading from the selection, click again on this heading. Click on *Properties* if you want to change the properties of the printer (Dialog box 18).

Send Mail

This option is available in an Output window only and can be used to send an e-mail with the whole output or parts of it.

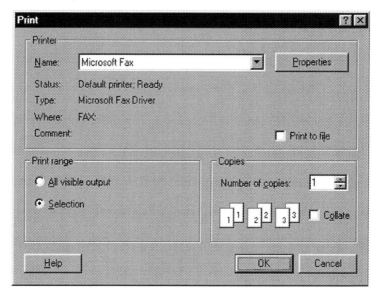

Dialog box 18

Export Output (Dialog box 19)

This option is available in an Output window only. You can use it to export text, tables, or charts to other applications. The exported items can be saved in an HTML or text format. Charts can be saved in a variety of picture formats. In the *Export* box specify which objects you want to export. In the *Export file* box specify where the output will be exported. Use the *Browse* button, if needed, to modify the destination. At the bottom of this dialog box select what you want to export; *All Objects* will export both hidden and visible parts of the output. Finally, select the *format* (i.e., type of file) that will be used to export the file.

Edit

Undo

SPSS will let you undo your last action only.

Find

This is a very useful option, especially if you have a large data file. For example, the data file below has 428 cases. If you are looking for an individual who was born on 19/11/83, click on the label of the *dob* (date of birth) column to highlight the whole column. In the *Find* dialog box type 19.11.83 and click *Find Next*. You will find that the particular date of birth corresponds to case No 359 (Figure 7).

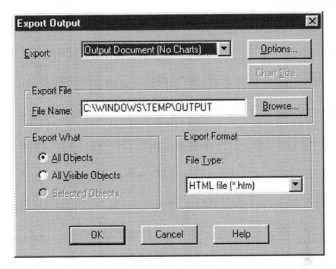

Dialog box 19

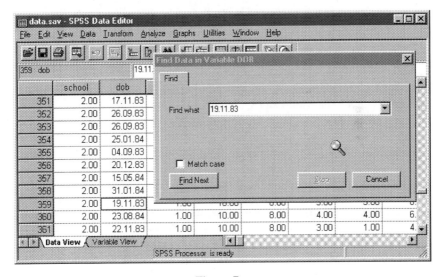

Figure 7

Options

SPSS offers a variety of options. In the *General* tab, under *Variable list*, select whether you want the dialog boxes to display the variables in an alphabetical order or in the order they are listed in the data file (*file*). You can also select whether you want the dialog boxes to display the names or the labels of the variables (see *Data entry* in Chapter 1). In the *Viewer* tab, tick the box *Display Commands in the Log*. SPSS will then present in the Output menu the commands for any analysis that you will subsequently carry out. The commands can be copied and pasted onto a Syntax file. In a future session, you can re-run the whole analysis from the Syntax file using the pasted commands. In this way you avoid saving the output file and all its tables and charts, which usually take up a lot of memory space. Of course, running the analysis from the Syntax window is recommended only to experienced SPSS users.

In the *Output Labels* tab, select *labels and names* or *values and labels*. Labels and names make the interpretation of output tables and charts easier. In the *Pivot Tables* tab, you may want to change the style of the tables to one of the *Academic Styles* offered. In the *Autoscripts* tab, you can select a number of autoscripts. Autoscripts are clusters of commands which are carried out automatically every time you perform a relevant analysis. For example, you may not like that, in a *bivariate correlation analysis* (see Chapter 3) the output table gives you the correlation coefficient between two variables in both the upper and lower diagonals. In this case, select the correlations autoscript. Next time you perform a correlation analysis SPSS will display the correlations in the lower diagonal only, and will highlight the highest correlation. In Table 2 you can see the correlation table before, and in Table 3 after, using the correlation autoscript. For more information on using scripts, see *Run Script* under the *Utilities* menu.

Outline

This option is available only in an Output window. *Promote* and *outline* arrange the headings and titles within a given block of the output. This option should be familiar to those who use the Outline view in Word.

Table 2

Correlations		competitive1	competition2	competition3	competition4
competitive1	Pearson Correlation	1.000	.308**	.328**	.237**
	Sig. (2-tailed)	.	.000	.000	.000
	N	419	415	419	419
competition2	Pearson Correlation	.308**	1.000	.381**	.305**
	Sig. (2-tailed)	.000	.	.000	.000
	N	415	421	421	421
competition3	Pearson Correlation	.328**	.381**	1.000	.280**
	Sig. (2-tailed)	.000	.000	.	.000
	N	419	421	426	426
competition4	Pearson Correlation	.237**	.305**	.280**	1.000
	Sig. (2-tailed)	.000	.000	.000	.
	N	419	421	426	426

**. Correlation is significant at the 0.01 level (2-tailed).

Table 3

		competitive1	competition2	competition3	competition4
Correlations					
competitive1	Pearson Correlation				
	Sig. (2-tailed)	.			
	N	419	415		
competition2	Pearson Correlation	.9**	1.000	.9**	
	Sig. (2-tailed)				
	N	415			
competition3	Pearson Correlation	.328**	.381**		
	Sig. (2-tailed)	.000	.000	.	
	N				
competition4	Pearson Correlation	.237**			
	Sig. (2-tailed)	.000	.000		
	N	419	421	426	

**. Correlation is significant at the 0.01 level (2-tailed).

SPSS Pivot Table Object or SPSS Chart Object

This option is available only in an Output window and it is activated when you click on a table or a chart. With this option you can modify the properties of a table or a chart. Select *Edit* or *Open* to open new menus with additional options.

View

Value Labels

If you tick *Value Labels*, you will be able to see the labels that you have assigned to the values of a variable. For example, for the 'gender' variable you may have used the value 1 to label females, and the value 2 to label males.

Expand/Collapse

These options are available only in an Output window. With these you can view all the different parts of an output block (e.g., title, notes, tables, and charts), or you can collapse the output and view a part of each block (e.g., the title) only. The *collapse* option is particularly useful for large output files. To activate these options you need to click on an output block.

Show/Hide

These options are available only in an Output Window. With *Show* you can view the hidden parts of an output (i.e., the notes). You need to click on an output block to activate these options.

Data

Define Dates

Use this option when the cases (rows) in the data file represent different points in time and not different individuals. With this option new variables are created in the data file which describe the periodicity of the data in a number of different ways. In the *Cases Are* box specify the type of time interval in the data. For example, assume that you have used appropriate equipment to record continuously the heart rate of a group of individuals every minute for two days. Select *days, hours, minutes* from the *Cases Are* box. In the *First Case Is* option, specify the starting date value of the data. Based on the first value and the type of time interval, the remaining cases will be assigned a specific date value. The numbers *24* and *60* next to *hour* and *minute* respectively indicate the maximum values you can enter.

Four new variables will appear in the data file: *day_*, *hour_*, *minute_*, and *date_* (Figure 8). The first three are self-explanatory; the fourth combines the day, hour, and minute of each observation (case) into one column. To remove the new variables from the date file, select *Not dated* in Dialog box 20.

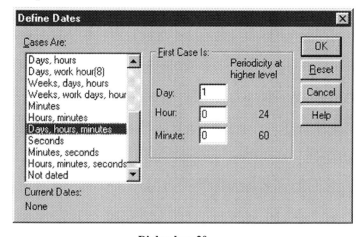

Dialog box 20

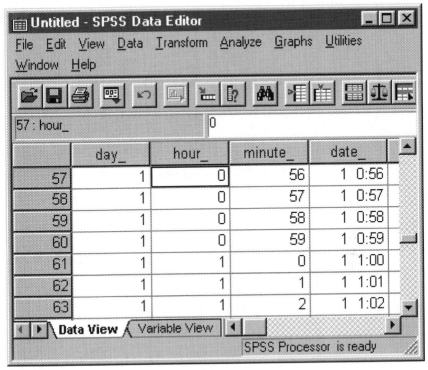

Figure 8

Insert Variable

If you want to insert a new variable (column) between two variables, click once on the label of one of the two columns in order to highlight it, and then choose the *Insert Variable* option. A new column will appear in the data file.

Insert Case

If you want to insert a new row (e.g., one questionnaire you forgot to enter) between two rows, highlight one of the two rows by clicking once on its number, and then choose the *Insert Case* option.

Go to Case

This option is useful if you have a large data file and you want to go directly to a particular case (participant). Type the case number and click OK.

Sort Cases (Dialog box 21)

You can use this option to sort the values of one or more variables in an ascending or descending order. For example, you can use this option to sort in an

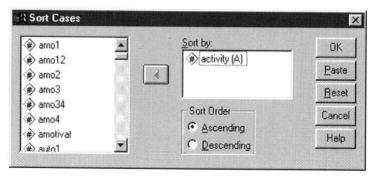

Dialog box 21

ascending order the values that have been assigned to the main sport of a group of pupils. As a result, all pupils who do aerobics will appear first (1 is the code given to aerobics), followed by all pupils whose sport has been assigned the code 2, etc. Using this option you can group together all pupils who practise a particular sport. Of course, you can use more than one variable to sort out the cases. For example, by using *activity* and *gender*, you can group separately all the females and all the males who do aerobics.

Transpose (Dialog box 22)

With this option you can create a new data file in which the rows and the columns of the old file are transposed in the new file, so that the rows become columns and vice versa. Move all the variables of the old file into the *Variable(s)* box; otherwise they will not appear in the new data file. If the old file contains a variable whose values could be used as variable names in the new data file, move this variable into the *Name Variable* box.

Figure 9 shows the results when seven long-jumpers were tested on four trials.

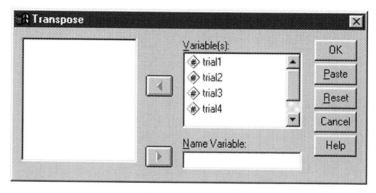

Dialog box 22

	trial1	trial2	trial3	trial4
1	7.86	7.89	7.84	7.56
2	8.02	8.00	7.95	7.84
3	8.23	8.25	8.04	8.07
4	7.45	7.48	7.85	7.58
5	7.89	7.98	8.04	8.14
6	8.01	8.06	7.84	8.09
7	8.41	8.45	8.31	8.29

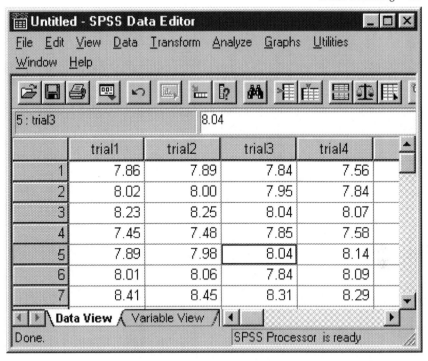

Figure 9

Figure 10 shows the new transposed file. The four trials are now represented in rows and the scores of the seven long jumpers are now represented in columns.

Often, in a dialog box you will need to select more than one variable. To select multiple consecutive variables press Shift on the keyboard, and while pressing, click with the mouse on the appropriate variables. To select multiple non-consecutive variables press Control on the keyboard, and while pressing, click on the appropriate variables. To remove a variable from the selection, click again on this variable.

	case_lbl	var001	var002	var003	var004	var005	var006	var007
1	TRIAL1	7.86	8.02	8.23	7.45	7.89	8.01	8.41
2	TRIAL2	7.89	8.00	8.25	7.48	7.98	8.06	8.45
3	TRIAL3	7.84	7.95	8.04	7.85	8.04	7.84	8.31
4	TRIAL4	7.56	7.84	8.07	7.58	8.14	8.09	8.29

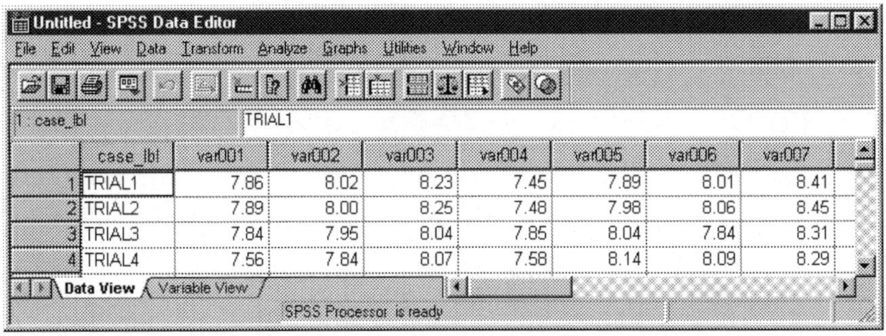

Figure 10

Merge File (Add Cases)

This option is useful when you want to combine two different data files. Suppose you have collected some additional questionnaires and you have saved them in a file called study3. You want to add these questionnaires to an older file called study2. Open study2, thus making it your working data file. Select the *Merge File, Add Cases* option. Find study3 and click *OK* (Dialog box 23).

At the right of this dialog box you can see the questions that participants answered in both studies 2 and 3 (*eff1–eff4*). At the left of this dialog box you can see the *unpaired variables*, that is, the variables that were answered in study2 (*) only, or in study 3 (+) only. If you want the merged file to contain all the unpaired variables, highlight them and move them into the *Variables in New Working Data File* box. If you want to indicate in the merged data file where the common variables (*eff1–eff4*) came from, tick the *Indicate case source as variable* option. This will create a new variable in the merged data file called *source 01* (Figure 11). This variable will show, for example, that the first 428 answers on *eff1–eff4* came from study2 (which has been assigned the code 0 by SPSS), and the remaining answers came from study3 (which has been assigned the code 1).

Merge File (Add Variables)

Add Variables (Dialog box 24) merges the working data file (study2) with another data file (study1) that contains the same cases but different variables. For example, you might want to merge two data files which contain different measures on the same individuals. Open study2, thus making it the working data file. Find study1 and click *OK*. Select the *Merge File, Add Cases* option.

The *New Working Data File* box indicates the variables that the new merged file will contain. As you can see, none of the variables was measured in both studies, and therefore, the *Excluded Variables* box is empty.

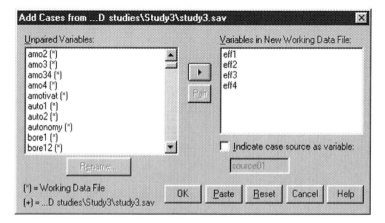

Dialog box 23

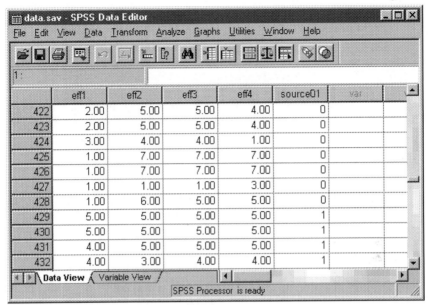

Figure 11

Dialog box 24

Split File (Dialog box 25)

This option is similar to the *Sort Cases* option described above. For example, by selecting *Compare groups* and moving *gender* and *level* in the *Groups based on* box, the data file will be sorted by each level of participation within the male and female groups. That is, the data will be sorted in a way that all males who

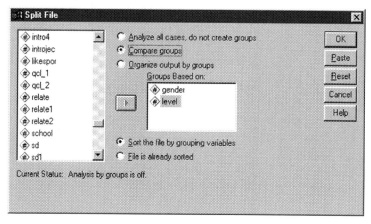

Dialog box 25

Table 4

Correlations

GENDER	LEVEL				GOALS	POWER
females	recreational	GOALS	Pearson Correlation		1.000	.124
			Sig. (2-tailed)		.	.
			N		25	25
		POWER	Pearson Correlation		.124	1.000
			Sig. (2-tailed)		.	.
			N		25	25
	competitive	GOALS	Pearson Correlation		1.000	.668**
			Sig. (2-tailed)		.	.
			N		25	25
		POWER	Pearson Correlation		.668**	1.000
			Sig. (2-tailed)		.	.
			N		25	25
males	recreational	GOALS	Pearson Correlation		1.000	.287
			Sig. (2-tailed)		.	.
			N		25	25
		POWER	Pearson Correlation		.287	1.000
			Sig. (2-tailed)		.	.
			N		25	25
	competitive	GOALS	Pearson Correlation		1.000	.756**
			Sig. (2-tailed)		.	.
			N		25	25
		POWER	Pearson Correlation		.756**	1.000
			Sig. (2-tailed)		.	.
			N		25	25

are recreational footballers will be presented first, followed by all male competitive footballers, all female recreational footballers, and finally by all female competitive footballers.

With this option, the results of any analysis (e.g., correlation between leg power and goal scoring) will be presented separately for the four groups (Table 4).

If you change your mind and you do not want to *compare groups*, select the *Analyze all cases, do not create groups* option.

Select Cases (Dialog box 26)

Suppose you want to analyse separately those pupils who do aerobics. How do you separate them from the rest of the sample? You need to use the *Select Cases* option. Click on the variable of interest (i.e., *activity*) and then select the option *If condition is satisfied*. Click on the *If...* button and you will be presented with Dialog box 27.

Now, select the variable *activity* and click on the arrow button to move it to the opposite box. Because you are interested only in those who do aerobics, type *activity = 1* (1 is the code given for aerobics). Click on *Continue* and you will get back to Dialog box 26. Click *OK*. As you can see, SPSS has selected in the data file only those pupils who do aerobics and you can use their data for further analysis. The responses of all other pupils have been filtered, as indicated by the slash through each unselected row number (Figure 12). The filter status is also indicated in the data file with a new variable (FILTER_$), which uses the value

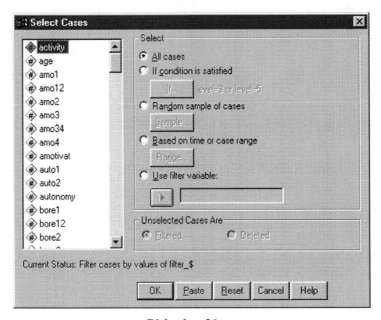

Dialog box 26

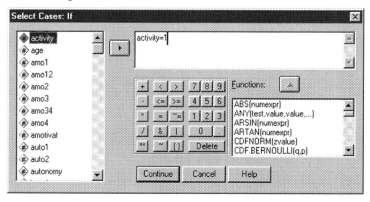

Dialog box 27

Figure 12

of 1 for selected cases and the value of 0 for unselected cases. To select all cases again, click *Select all cases* at the top of Dialog box 26.

If you want to analyse, say, only the first 50 participants, select *Based on time or range case* and click on *Range*. In the new dialog box indicate that you are interested in the first 50 cases only (Dialog box 28).

At the bottom of Dialog box 26, you can specify whether you want the unselected cases to be *filtered* or *deleted*. It is preferable not to delete them, because you may need them later on in other analyses. In Figure 12, the unselected cases were filtered.

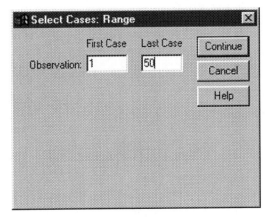

Dialog box 28

Weight Cases (Dialog box 29)

This option is especially useful when you want to carry out a chi-square test (see *Nonparametric Tests-Chi Square* in the *Analyze* menu). Usually, a cell in a data file represents one observation for a particular case. However, on some occasions you may want a cell to represent the frequency of occurrence of cases of a particular variable. In Figure 13 the column *frequenc* shows that 100 pupils differ in their choice of favourite football club: 32 pupils support club A, 26 support club B, 19 support club C, 14 support club D, and 9 support club E.

Weight cases will tell SPSS that the values in the cells represent frequencies of occurrence of cases and not individual cases. Move *frequenc* into the *Frequency Variable* box and click *OK*.

As you can see, the cases of only one variable (i.e., support for a particular football club) can be weighted. A note will appear at the bottom of the data file which will remind you that the cases have been weighted. If you subsequently weight the cases of another variable, the case weighting of the original variable will be turned off. You can also turn off the case weighting of a variable by selecting *Do not weight cases.*

Transform

Compute

This option is very useful and can be used in many different ways. For example, it lets you create a new column (variable) in the data file which represents the mean scores of other columns. Suppose you have five different items that measure competence and you want to create a new column which represents the mean score of these items. Under *Target Variable*, type the name of the new variable (e.g., *competen*). Then choose the *Mean function*, click on the arrow

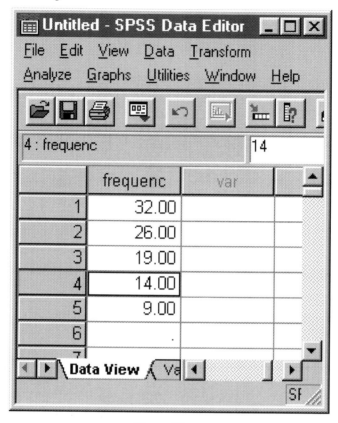

Figure 13

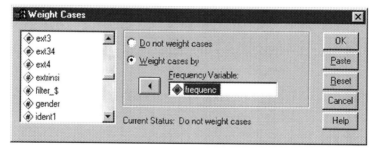

Dialog box 29

button, and move the variable in the *Numeric Expression* box. Insert between the brackets all the competence items that are listed in the box on the left-hand side. Select one item at a time and use the arrow button to move it inside the brackets of the Mean function. Repeat this procedure until you have transferred across all the competence items. Separate each item with a comma. Finally, click *OK*. A

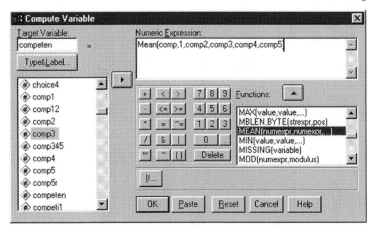

Dialog box 30

new variable (column) will appear in the data file showing the mean scores of all five competence items. In a similar way, other *numeric expressions* can also be used to compute a new variable which will represent, for example, the sum or the product of existing variables (Dialog box 30).

Compute is also useful when you want to create a new variable which will code the cases of an existing variable into different groups (useful for parametric *t* tests, ANOVA, and MANOVA; see the *Analyze* menu). Suppose you want to code an intention to do physical activity (*intent*) variable into two groups: those with high intention (code 1) and those with low intention (code 2). To split the variable into these two groups you need to find out its median value (see *Summarize Frequencies* in the *Analyze* menu below). Suppose the median value is 3.7 on a 1 ('I certainly do not intend to do exercise') to 5 ('I certainly intend to do exercise') continuum. The new variable will be named *intention groups,* or *intengro,* since you are restricted to 8 characters. In the *Numeric Expression* box, type 1 (Dialog box 31).

Click *If* at the bottom of the dialog box. In the new dialog box that appears (Dialog box 32) select *Include if case satisfies condition*. Move the variable *intent* in the upper right-hand box and type *intent>3.7*, because you want to assign the code 1 to those with high intention (i.e., those who score above the median). Click *OK*.

Now return to Dialog box 31. Click *OK* and a new variable will appear in the data file called *intengro* which contains the value 1. However, you also want to include in this variable those with low intention to exercise. Follow the same procedure by typing 2 in the *Numeric Expression* box of Dialog box 31. Then in Dialog box 32 type *intent* ≤ 3.7 (or *intent* < 3.7, if you do not want to include the median score). Click *Continue* and then *OK*. A new dialog box will appear (Dialog box 33) which will ask you whether you want to change the existing variable (i.e., *intengro*). Click *OK* because you want to change it so that it contains the values of both 1 and 2.

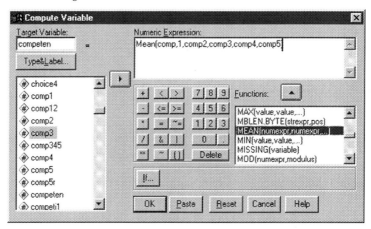

Dialog box 31

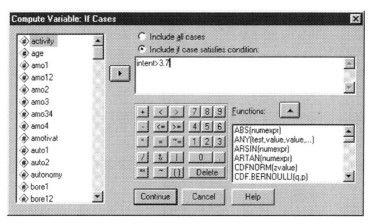

Dialog box 32

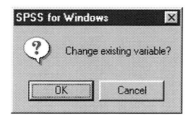

Dialog box 33

You can also use the *Compute* option to create a new categorical variable which will be the combination of two existing variables (useful for ANOVA and MANOVA; see the *Analyze* menu). Suppose you have measured the number of sit-ups and press-ups in 60 seconds of a group of athletes, and you want to create a new variable called *strength* which will combine the sit-up and press-up

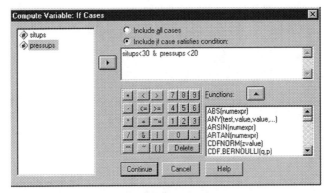

Dialog box 34

scores. This variable will assign the code of 1 to those athletes with scores higher than the median scores of both tests, 2 to those with high score on sit-ups and low score on press-ups, 3 to those with low sit-up/high press-up scores, and 4 to those with low sit-up/low press-up scores. Find the median scores of the two tests (see *Frequencies* in the *Statistics* menu) and follow the same procedure as in the example above. For instance, in order to create the low sit-up/low press-up group (assuming that the median score of sit-ups is 30 and of press-ups is 20) the dialog box should look like Dialog box 34.

Another very useful way of using the *Compute* option is to estimate the age of participants based on their date of birth. Suppose you have two columns in the data file, one which shows the date of birth (*dob*) of the participants and another which shows the date (*period*) they participated in your study. You may want to create another column, *age*, which will show their age when they took part in the study. Firstly, *dob*, and *period* should have a *date* type (see *Data entry* in Chapter 1). As you can see in Dialog box 35, in each cell of the *dob* and *period* variables dates should be entered in the form of day, month, and year (*dd.mm.yy*).

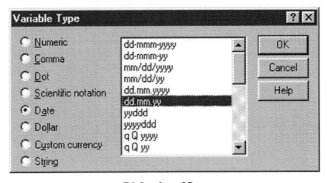

Dialog box 35

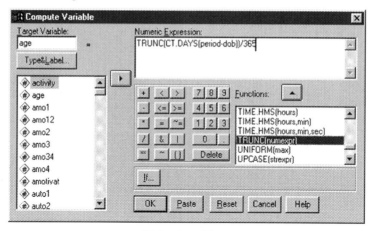

Dialog box 36

Go to the *Compute* option (Dialog box 36). Type *age* in the *Target Variable* box. The *Numeric Expression* is *TRUNC(CT.DAYS(period-dob))/365*. Click *OK* and a new column will appear in the data file containing the ages of the participants.

Count

With this option you can count the number of occurrences of a particular value across the different variables of the same case (individual) (Dialog box 37). Suppose you want to find out how many different sports are practised by a sample of pupils. In an available list of five sports (variables), type 1 if they practise a particular sport and 0 if they do not practise it. You want to find out how many different sports each pupil (case) practises. In other words, you want to find out how many 1s each pupil has reported. *Count* creates a new column

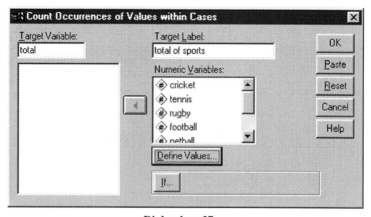

Dialog box 37

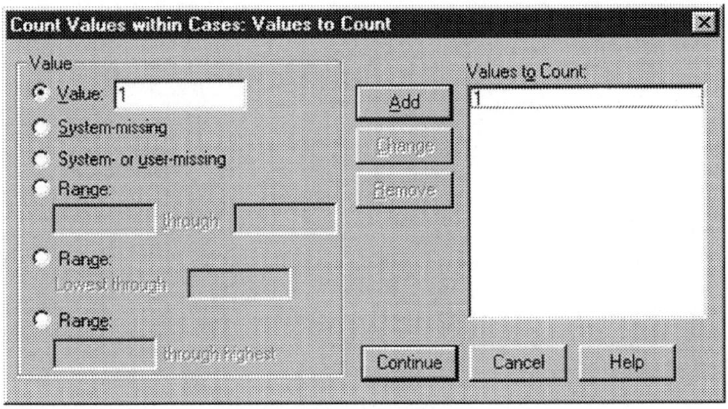

Dialog box 38

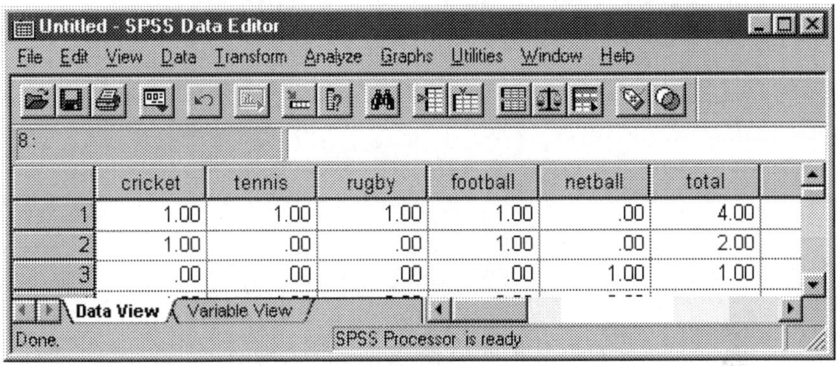

Figure 14

(variable) in the data file with the tally of all sports for each pupil. Name this variable *total*. Use the arrow to move all the sports in the *Numeric Variables* box.

Click on *Define Values*. In Dialog box 38 type 1 and click *Add* to move this value into the *Values to Count* box.

Click *Continue* and you will get back to Dialog box 37. Click *OK* and the new variable *total* will appear in the data file. As you can see, the first pupil participates in 4 of the 5 examined sports, whereas the last participant plays only one of these sports (Figure 14). To present the results in an appropriate table, see *Custom Tables/Multiple Response Tables* in the *Analyze* menu.

Recode into Same Variables (Dialog box 39)

You can recode the values of a variable and still retain this variable in a data file. For example, you may have used four variables to measure perceptions of competence. Three are positively worded (e.g., 'I feel competent') and are

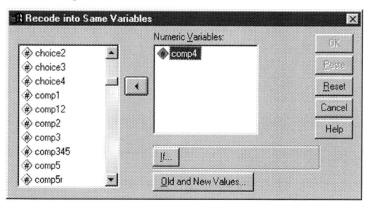

Dialog box 39

Dialog box 40

scored on a scale from 1–4 (1 = 'strongly disagree', 4 = 'strongly agree'). The fourth measure of perceived competence is negatively worded (e.g., 'I feel incompetent'), but it is also measured on a scale from 1–4. To be consistent with the other perceived competence variables, you need to recode the last variable so that, for example, all 1s are recoded into 4. In other words, those who strongly disagree that they are incompetent are indirectly strongly agreeing that they are competent. Select the fourth perceived competence variable and move it into the *Numeric Variables* box. Click *Old and New Values*.

Now you need to specify the old and the new values (Dialog box 40). Type the first old value (i.e., 1) into the *Old Value* box and the new corresponding value (i.e., 4) into the *New Value* box. When you finish, click *Add*.

Repeat this procedure until you have recoded all the old values. When you finish, click *Continue* and you will get back to Dialog box 39. Click *OK* and the original variable will be recoded into the same variable but will contain different values.

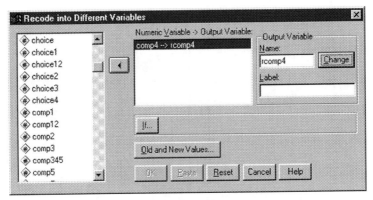

Dialog box 41

Recode into Different Variables (Dialog box 41)

In some cases you may want to recode the values of a variable but retain its original values. To achieve this, you need to recode the original variable into a different variable. Continuing from the previous example, you need to rename variable *comp4* into *rcomp4*. This procedure will create a new recoded variable in the data file without replacing the original one. Move the original *comp4* into the *Numeric Variable–>Output Variable* box. In the *Output Variable* box give a name to the new variable (e.g., recoded competence4, *rcomp4*) and click *Change*. Now, you can see in the dialog box the expression *comp4–>rcomp4*, that is, SPSS is ready to recode the *competence4* variable into a new variable. Click on *Old and New Values* and repeat the procedure outlined in the *Recode into Same Variables* option. Furthermore, if you want the new variable to use the same value (e.g., 9) as the old variable to indicate missing cases, you should also recode value 9 into value 9. A new variable will appear in the data file whose values are the recoded values of the original variable.

Categorize Variables (Dialog box 42)

With this option you can convert a continuous variable into a categorical one. Suppose you have recorded the improvement (*improvem*) in the aerobic capacity of a group of athletes after a specific training programme. You may be interested in classifying the athletes into four improvement groups (percentiles). Move *improvem* into the *Create Categories for* box. In the *Number of categories* box type *4* to indicate that you want to create four equal groups. Click *OK*.

A new categorical variable will appear in the data file called *nimprove* (Figure 15). This variable has four values ranging from 1, which represents those athletes with the maximum aerobic capacity improvement, to 4, which indicates the athletes with the minimum aerobic capacity improvement.

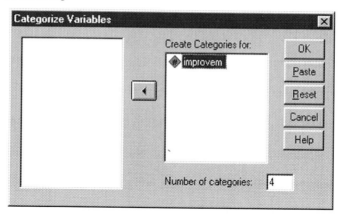

Dialog box 42

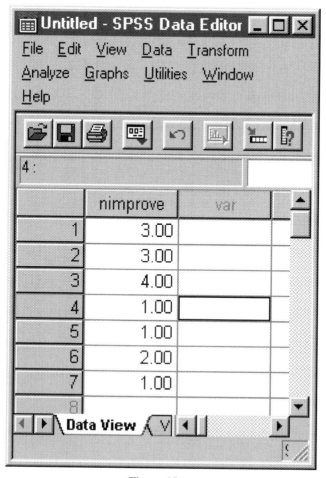

Figure 15

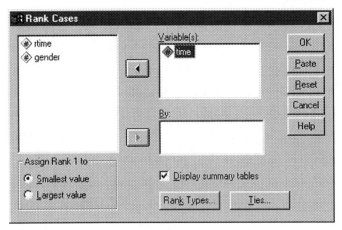

Dialog box 43

Rank Cases (Dialog box 43)

This option is useful when you want to convert raw data into meaningful ranks. For example, suppose you have conducted a 40m-sprint test and you have recorded the participants' times. You may want to rank them starting from the fastest runner. Select the variable *time* and move it into the *Variable(s):* box. Click *OK* and a new variable will appear in the data file called *rtime*, which has ranked all runners starting from the fastest (who has been allocated rank 1). Depending on the type of data, you may want to assign rank 1 to the largest rather than the smallest value (e.g., results from a strength test). Therefore, make the most appropriate selection when using the *Assign Rank 1 to* option. Note that ties are assigned the same rank.

In the example shown in Dialog box 43, you may want to rank the participants within subgroups (e.g., gender). That is, you may want to find out who is the fastest among males (code 1) and among females (code 2). The fastest from both groups will be assigned rank 1. In addition to what you did before, you need to move the *gender* variable into the *By* box. In the example shown in Figure 16, *rtime* is the new variable which contains the ranks for males and females.

As you can see, the fastest male ran in 5.01 seconds and the fastest female in 5.62 seconds. Both have rank 1 in the *rtime* column, because the runners have been ranked within their gender group.

Replace Missing Values (Dialog box 44)

Most types of research, especially those involving questionnaires, have to deal with the problem of missing values. Some participants may not understand certain questions, or they may overlook them, or even consciously decide not to answer them. Incomplete questionnaires pose a problem, especially if the sample

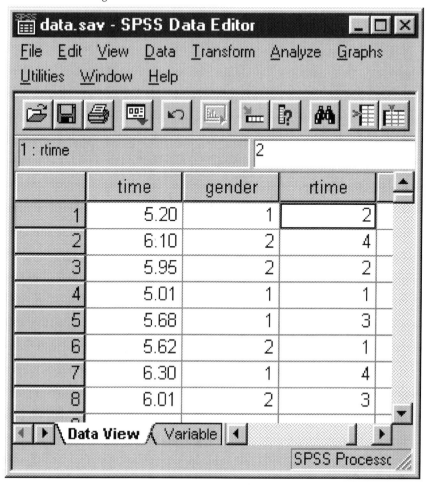

Figure 16

size of a survey is small. SPSS will ignore the missing values (indicated by empty cells or by a specific code; see *Data Entry* in Chapter 1), unless you decide to replace them. Suppose some patients decide not to answer a question regarding their monthly attendance at an exercise programme of a cardiac rehabilitation centre. Find the variable *attend* and move it into the *New Variable(s)* box. SPSS by default will use the *Series mean* method to calculate the missing values and will create a new variable with no missing values called *attend_1*. If you do not like the new name you can change it by clicking on *Change*. When you finish, click *OK* and a new column will appear in the data file called *attend_1*. This column has all the monthly attendance scores without any missing values.

The *Series mean* method replaces the missing values with the mean score of the particular variable (i.e., *attend*). This is the most common method of

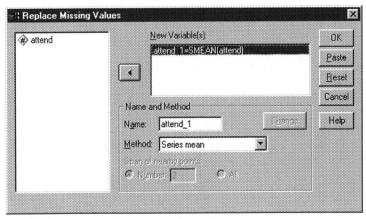

Dialog box 44

replacing missing values. The *Mean of nearby points* method substitutes the missing values with the mean scores of valid (i.e., non-missing) surrounding values. Use the *Span of nearby points* to specify whether you want to include a certain *Number* of nearby points or *All* valid nearby points. In a similar way, the *Median of nearby points* method replaces the missing values with the median score of valid surrounding values.

3   Statistical tests

Analyze

A variety of different table styles and their options are described in this chapter. In addition to these options, some additional ones relating to table format will appear when you double-click any of the tables below. For a detailed discussion of these additional options, see Chapter 4.

Reports/OLAP (Online Analytical Processing) Cubes (Dialog box 45)

Use this option to produce summary statistics (e.g., means, standard deviations, maximum and minimum values) for a continuous variable within the different levels of a categorical variable. For example, suppose you have measured the heart rate of two groups of athletes. Move the continuous variable *heartrat* into the *Summary Variable(s)* box and the categorical variable *groups* into the *Grouping Variable(s)* box.

Click *Statistics* to select the descriptive statistics to be displayed (Dialog box 46).

For the example shown in Table 5, select *Mean, Standard Deviation, Minimum,* and *Maximum.* Click *Continue* and you will go back to Dialog box 45. Click *Title* to label the output table. Then click *OK.*

As you can see, SPSS has produced the overall statistics for both groups, as well as separate statistics for each group. Use the drop-down list to see the results for each group. For more advanced tables, see *Custom Tables* below.

Descriptive Statistics/Frequencies (Dialog box 47)

Use this option when you want to calculate descriptive statistics for different variables. Select the variables of interest and move them into the *Variable(s)* box. Tick the *Display frequency tables* box, and the Output window will present a detailed frequency table for each selected variable (e.g., a breakdown of age groups).

Click *Statistics.* Select some of the most commonly used descriptive statistics, such as the *mean* and *standard deviation.* The *minimum* and *maximum*

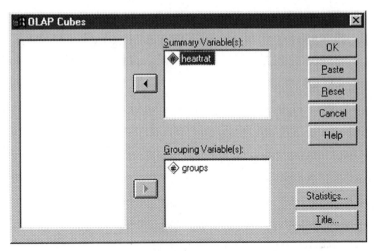

Dialog box 45

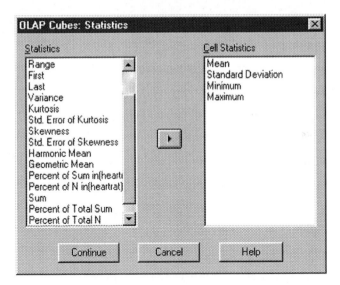

Dialog box 46

values are very important when you want to detect potential inaccuracies in data entry (Dialog box 48). Usually, you have a pretty good idea of what should be the minimum and maximum scores of a variable, especially if you have used close-ended questions. Any out-of-range values (e.g., the value 11 on a question where possible answers range from 1 to 5) can be detected and corrected here. *Skewness* and *kurtosis* are useful in assessing the normality of the data. If the ratio of *skewness* or *kurtosis* to their respective *standard errors* is above 1.96, the data are probably not normally distributed.

Table 5

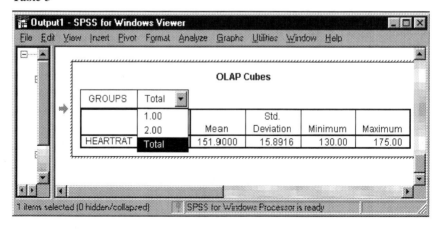

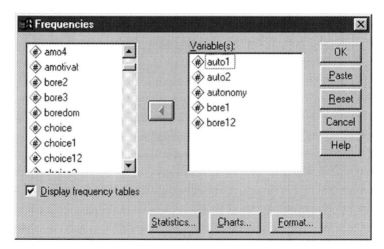

Dialog box 47

In Dialog box 48 you can also specify *cut-off points to create equal groups*. For example, if you want to create six extrinsic motivation groups with equal numbers in each group, the Output window will give you the values of five different percentiles (i.e., 100/6: 16.66, 33.33, 50, 66.66 and 83.33). As you can see in the output table, the first group has values below 2 on the extrinsic motivation scale, because 2 is the cut-off point for the first percentile. The second group has values greater than 2 and smaller than 3, because 2 and 3 are the cut-off points for the 16.66 and 33.33 percentiles, etc. You can use the cut-off points to create a new variable in the data file with values corresponding to each of the six groups (see *Transform* in the *Compute* menu).

If you are interested in examining in detail a specific percentile, you can type its value in the *Percentile(s)* box of Dialog box 48 and then click *Add*. For

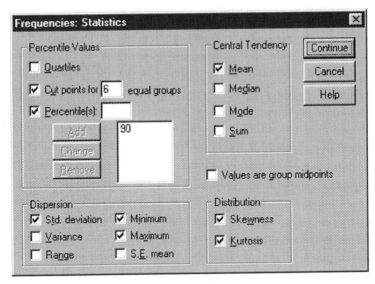

Dialog box 48

example, if you are interested in the 90th percentile, that is, in those individuals whose scores on extrinsic motivation are higher than 90% of the sample, the Output window will tell you that these individuals have a score of 7 on the extrinsic motivation scale. *Quartiles* present the values for the 25th, 50th, and 75th percentile, that is, they give the cut-off points for 4 equal groups (Table 6).

In Dialog box 47 click *Charts*. For each selected variable, SPSS can produce either *a bar chart, a pie chart* or *a histogram*. The values in the charts can represent the number of cases (*frequencies*) or the *percentage* of cases for each category of a variable (e.g., number of males and females) (Dialog box 49).

Click *Continue* and you will get back to Dialog box 47. Then click *Format*. Here you can specify how you want the values of the selected variables to appear in the frequency tables (Dialog box 50).

For example, a frequency table showing the main sport of a group of pupils can be *ordered by ascending or descending values*. Note that you must have assigned a value to each sport in the data file, for example, 1 to aerobics, 2 to badminton, etc. The frequency list can also be sorted starting from the least popular sport (*ascending counts*) or the most popular sport (*descending counts*). Note that all sports should be in one column in the data file with the name *activity*.

If you would like to present the descriptive statistics (e.g., *M, SD*) of the *activity* variable at the bottom of Table 7, select the Statistics Table (i.e., Table 6) and go to *Run Script* in the *Utilities* Menu. Select the *Frequencies footnote.sbs* and click *Run*. Another useful script is the *Make totals bold. sbs*. For more information on using scripts, see the *Utilities* Menu in Chapter 5.

In Dialog box 50 you can also indicate whether you want SPSS to present the descriptive statistics of all variables in one table (*compare variables*), or separately

Table 6

Statistics

extrinsic

N	Valid	425
	Missing	3
Mean		3.5347
Std. Deviation		1.6849
Skewness		.343
Std. Error of Skewness		.118
Kurtosis		-.735
Std. Error of Kurtosis		.236
Minimum		1.00
Maximum		7.00
Percentiles	16.66666667	1.7500
	33.33333333	2.5000
	50	3.5000
	66.66666667	4.0000
	83.33333333	5.2500
	90	6.2500

for each variable (*organize output by variables*). Some variables may contain a very wide range of categories (e.g., dates of birth) which make frequency tables meaningless. In such cases, indicate the maximum number of *categories* you want to examine at the bottom of Dialog box 50. SPSS will not produce a frequency table if a variable has more categories than the ones you specified.

Descriptive Statistics/Descriptives (Dialog box 51)

Use this option to create standardised scores (z scores) for a number of variables. Select the variables you are interested in and move them into the *Variable(s)* box. Tick the *Save standardized values as variables* box. Then, click *Options*.

Dialog box 49

Dialog box 50

Dialog box 51

Similar to the *Summarize Frequencies* option, you can ask for some descriptive statistics (Dialog box 52).

The output will display the variables in the order they appear in the data file (*variable list*), *alphabetically*, or starting with the variable with the lowest or

Table 7

ACTIVITY^a

		Frequency	Percent	Valid Percent	Cumulative Percent
Valid	Aerobics	34	7.9	8.0	8.0
	Badminton	44	10.3	10.4	18.4
	Football	98	22.9	23.2	41.6
	Athletics	71	16.6	16.8	58.4
	Trampoline	37	8.6	8.7	67.1
	Cricket	51	11.9	12.1	79.2
	Tennis	58	13.6	13.7	92.9
	Rounders	30	7.0	7.1	100.0
	Total	423	98.8	100.0	
Missing	9.00	5	1.2		
Total		428	100.0		

a. Valid = 423 Missing = 5 Mean = 4.34 Std. Deviation = 2.05 Skewness = .20 Kurtosis = -1.04 Minimum = 1 Maximum = 8

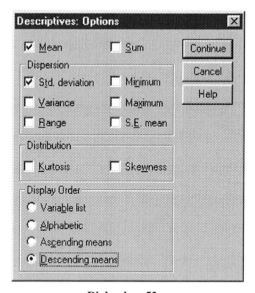

Dialog box 52

highest mean (*ascending or descending means*). The difference between this option and the *Summarize Frequencies* option, is that in the latter option different categories of the <u>same</u> variable are presented in an ascending or descending order, whereas in the *Summarize Descriptives* option the ascending and descending display orders are applied to <u>different</u> variables. *Summarize*

Table 8

Descriptive Statistics

	N	Mean	Std. Deviation
enjoyment	428	4.9866	1.4645
confiden	428	4.6986	1.6596
anxiety	425	3.6753	1.6290
Valid N (listwise)	425		

Descriptives is especially useful when you want to compare a large number of variables measured on the same scale. Table 8 is an example of *descending means display order* of three variables, enjoyment, confidence, and anxiety measured on a scale ranging from 1 to 6.

Descriptive Statistics/Explore (Dialog box 53)

Before you carry out any statistical analysis, it is recommended that you use this option to detect out-of-range values, to look for extreme but within-range values (i.e., outliers), and to test various assumptions of statistical tests. Select the variables you want to analyse and move them in the *Dependent List* box. If you want to analyse the variables separately for the different levels of a *Factor* (e.g., separately for males and females), identify a categorical variable with a few groups and place it into the *Factor List* box. For example, you may want to examine gender differences in the enjoyment of a fitness class. Click on *Statistics* to ask for descriptive statistics, particularly for *outliers* which can violate the assumptions of parametric tests. If no variables are identified in the *Factor List* box, the descriptive statistics will be displayed for the whole sample.

Click on *Plots* to indicate whether you want *Boxplots, Histograms*, or *Stem-and Leafs* plots (Dialog box 54).

Boxplots can be presented in two ways. Assume that you have two different measures of enjoyment. If you select the *Factor levels together* option, SPSS will plot two different boxplots, one for each measure. If you select the *Dependents together* option, SPSS will plot the two boxplots side-by-side, as illustrated in Figure 17.

The box shows the range of 50% of the cases of each variable. The thick line in the middle of the box indicates the median of the variable. The vertical lines extend to the highest and lowest values, excluding outliers. The circles at the bottom of the chart identify the outliers.

Dialog box 53

Dialog box 54

The *normality plots* or Q-Q plots give a graphical representation of the extent to which the data do not depart from normality, that is, the extent to which the little boxes in Figure 18 cluster around the straight line.

SPSS can also produce statistical tests of normality. Select *normality plots with tests* in Dialog box 54. If the *Kolmogorov-Smirnov* and *Shapiro-Wilk* tests are not significant, the assumption of normality is met. However, bear in mind that with small sample sizes the tests may not be significant, even if the normality assumption is wrong. Conversely, if the sample size is very large, the tests will be significant even if there are only mild deviations from normality (Table 9).

Options in Dialog box 53 offers choices regarding the handling of missing values. You can exclude from all analyses participants who have missing values

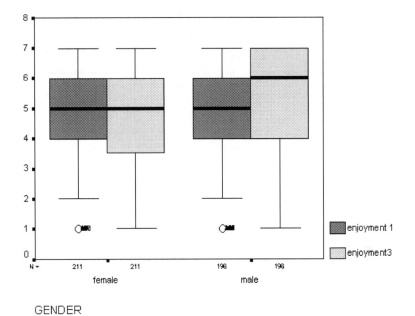

GENDER

Figure 17

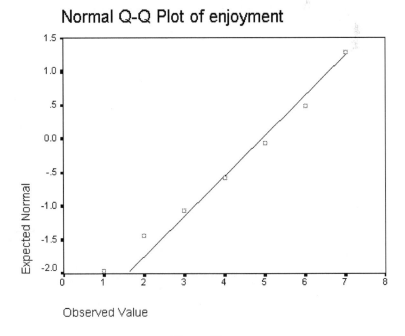

Figure 18

Table 9

Tests of Normality

	Kolmogorov-Smirnov[a]			Shapiro-Wilk		
	Statistic	df	Sig.	Statistic	df	Sig.
enjoyment	.187	30	.009	.917	30	.029

a. Lilliefors Significance Correction

(i.e., *listwise deletion*), or you can exclude those participants who have missing values in the variables that are used for a particular analysis (i.e., *pairwise deletion*). With *pairwise deletion*, the same participants can be used in another analysis that uses different (complete) variables. *Listwise deletion* can potentially result in a substantial decrease of sample size. Lastly, you can treat the missing values as a separate category and *report its values*.

Descriptive Statistics/Crosstabs (Dialog box 55)

Crosstabulations are very useful because they provide information regarding the breakdown of the sample. For example, in a survey of sports performers you can find out how many males and females practise a number of different sports. Select two or more variables and place them in the *Row(s)* or the *Column(s)* boxes. Although the variables can be placed in either of the two boxes, for practical purposes it is advisable to place variables with several categories in the

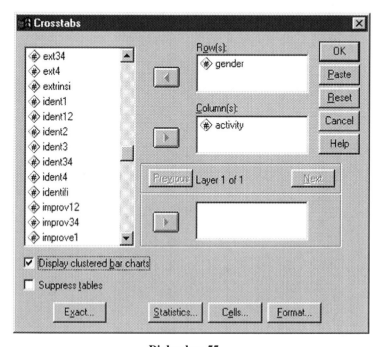

Dialog box 55

Table 10

GENDER * ACTIVITY Crosstabulation

Count

		GENDER		
		female	male	Total
ACTIVITY	Aerobics	30	4	34
	Badminton	8	36	44
	Football	50	47	97
	Athletics	20	51	71
	Trampoline	23	12	35
	Cricket		50	50
	Tennis	54	4	58
	Rounders	30		30
Total		215	204	419

Row(s) box. If you want a visual display of the crosstabulations, select the *Display clustered bar charts* option. Table 10 is an example of a gender by activity crosstabulation table.

If you want a further breakdown of the sample, select one or more categorical variables (e.g., age groups) and place them in the *Layer* box. In Table 10, you may want to find out how many 15-year-old and 17-year-old females play basketball. *Statistics* in Dialog box 55 provides crosstabulation results which may be of interest to advanced SPSS users. With *Cells* you can specify whether you want to display percentages for every row and column. *Format* specifies the presentation order of the variables.

Custom Tables/Basic Tables (Dialog box 56)

This option produces statistics for several subgroups in a more sophisticated fashion compared to *Reports/OLAP (Online Analytical Processing) Cubes* and *Descriptive Crosstabs* options in the *Analyze menu*. Suppose you have a measure of boredom and you want to examine how its descriptive statistics differ across activity and gender. Move the continuous variable *boredom1* into the *Summaries* box, and the two categorical variables (*activity* and *gender*) into the *Subgroups* boxes. It is up to you to decide whether a categorical variable will be displayed *Down* or *Across* in the output.

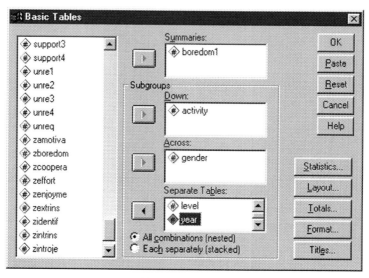

Dialog box 56

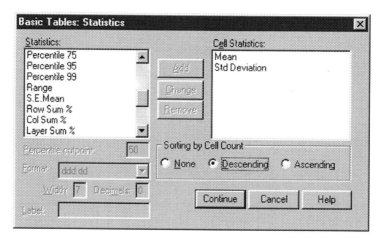

Dialog box 57

In Dialog box 56 click on *Statistics* to select the descriptive statistics that will be displayed in the output (Dialog box 57). Use the *Add* button to move the selected statistics in the *Cell Statistics* box. Similar to other options described earlier, you can choose whether you want the variables to be displayed in a *descending* or *ascending* order. When you finish click *Continue*.

Layout in Dialog box 56 lets you specify your preferences for the appearance of tables. The *Totals* option is useful when you want to show the totals for each group variable (in our example *activity* and *gender*). With *Format* you can

Table 11

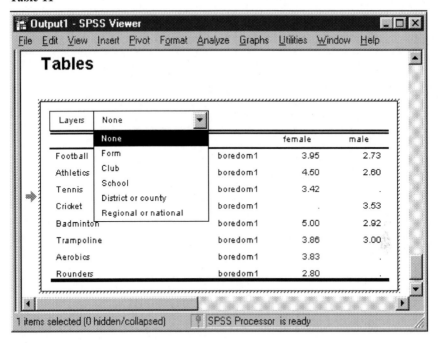

specify the appearance of missing values and statistics. Click *Titles* to provide titles to the table.

The *Separate Tables* box of Dialog box 56 allows a further breakdown of the sample across different clustered tables. For example, you can move into this box the variable *level* which indicates the competitive level of the sample. The output will display a table with a gender by activity breakdown of boredom scores. These scores will be presented in a descending order. Double-click on the table to see the *level* breakdown. Different competitive levels have a different gender by activity breakdown of boredom scores (Table 11).

Suppose you add a second variable in the *Separate Tables* box of Dialog box 56, the year of study of the pupils. The output can be displayed in two ways (see the bottom of Dialog box 56). Choose *nested* to group the years of study under each competitive level (Table 12).

You can also group the years of study independent of the competitive levels (*stacked*). In the example shown in Table 13, all competitive levels are displayed first, followed by the different years of study.

Custom Tables/General Tables (Dialog box 58)

General Tables can also be used to produce statistics for different subgroups. The selected variables can be either categorical (*Defines cells* under *Selected Variable*) such as different years of study, or they can represent a summary of

Table 12

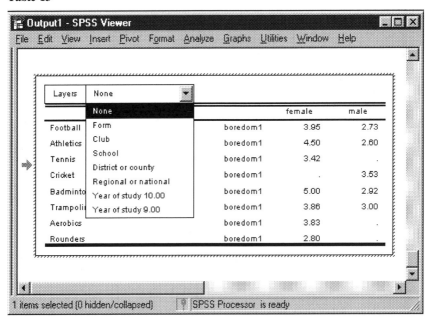

Table 13

other variables such as a scale average (*Is summarized* under *Selected Variable*). Click *Edit Statistics* to select the descriptive statistics that will be displayed in the output. Depending on the type of the selected variable (*defines cells,* or *is summarized*) the list of available statistics may differ. Click *Insert Total* if you want to display the total score for each of the selected variables. *Format* and

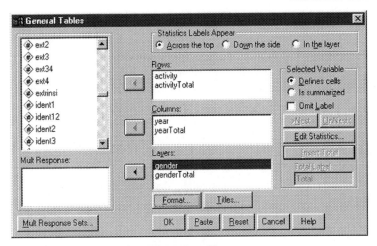

Dialog box 58

Table 14

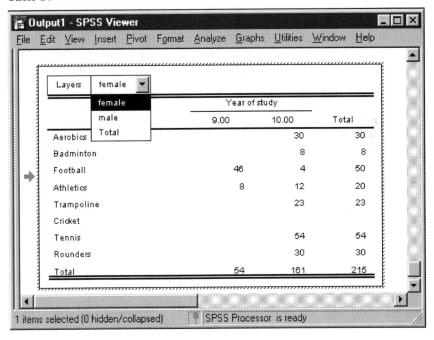

Titles work as in the *Basic Tables* option. Again, to see the different layers in the table, you need to double-click and open the table (Table 14).

Mult Response Sets at the bottom left-hand corner of Dialog box 58 will be described in the *Multiple Response Tables* option.

Custom Tables/Multiple Response Tables

This option allows you to build multiple response sets. These sets contain a group of variables which share a common characteristic (e.g., different types of sport). Similar to the examples described previously, a competitive level by gender crosstabulation will be displayed for each type of sport. However, there is one important difference. In the examples used previously, participants were asked to indicate their <u>main</u> sport, which means that there was <u>one</u> *activity* variable in the data file with many different categories (e.g., code 1 indicated aerobics, etc...) (Figure 19).

With *Multiple Response Tables*, participants are asked to indicate which sports they play from a list of available sports, and therefore, they can select <u>more than one</u> sport (see also *Count* in the *Transform* menu). In other words,

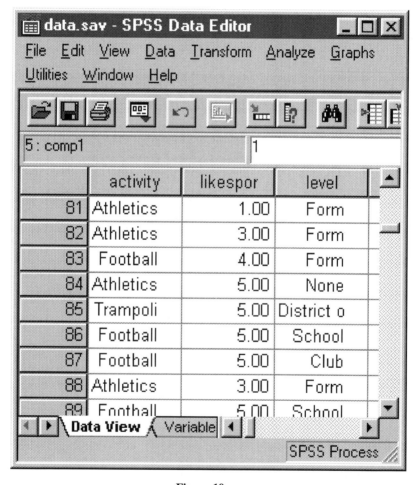

Figure 19

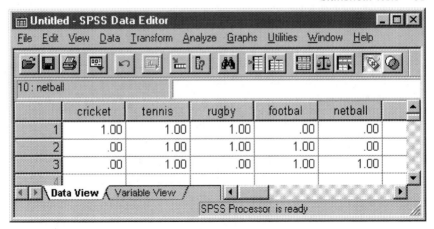

Figure 20

each sport appears as a separate variable (column) in the data file. Code 1 indicates that a participant plays a particular sport and code 0 indicates that he/she does not play this sport (Figure 20).

A multiple response set will be created for the different sports called *$sport*. Click *Define Sets* (Dialog box 59).

The *counted value* is 1 because this value indicates that a participant plays a particular sport. Give a brief name (*Name*) or a detailed name (*Label*) to the multiple response set and click *Add* (Dialog box 60).

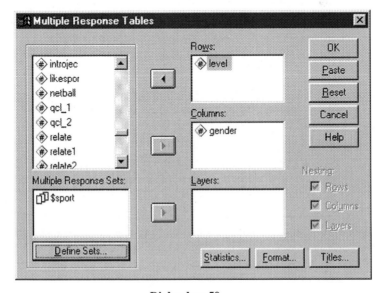

Dialog box 59

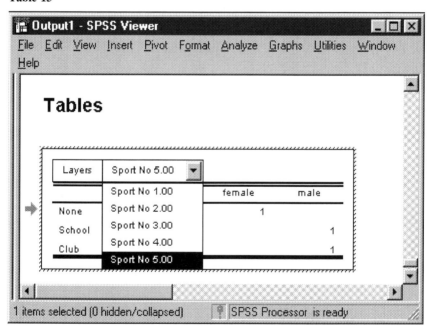

Dialog box 60

Table 15

If you do not want to create another set, click *Save* and you will get back to Dialog box 59. Move the new variable *$sport* into the *Layers* box. The *Statistics, Format*, and *Title* options work as in the previous tables. Click *OK* and the output will be displayed. Again, you need to double-click the table to view the different layers (Table 15).

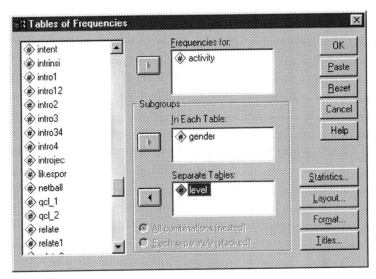

Dialog box 61

Custom Tables/Tables of Frequencies (Dialog box 61)

The *Tables of Frequencies* are in many respects similar to the other types of tables described above. You can request a table showing the frequencies for each category of a variable which appears in the *Frequencies for* box. Alternatively, you may break down the frequencies count according to some grouping variables such as gender and level of participation. The options at the bottom of this dialog box are very similar to the ones described in Dialog box 56. For an explanation of the *nested* and *stacked* options, see Table 12 and Table 13. Double-click the table to see the different layers (Table 16).

Compare Means/Means (Dialog box 62)

This option estimates the mean or other descriptive statistics of dependent variables (situated in the *Dependent List*) across the different subgroups of independent variables (located in the *Independent List*). You can create one or more *layers* or blocks of independent variables using the *Previous* and *Next* buttons. Each layer can include as many variables as you like. Use *Options* to specify which descriptive statistics you want to calculate.

In Table 17 two layers have been specified: frequency of exercise (*frequenc*) and gender. The latter variable will appear if you click on the *Next* button. Click *OK* to produce the output table. Table 17 shows the descriptive statistics for males and females (i.e., two subgroups of the first layer), as well as for those who exercise frequently or occasionally (i.e., two subgroups of the second layer), on a measure of body fat percentage.

Table 16

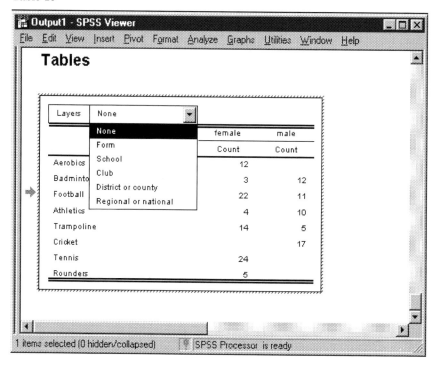

Dialog box 62

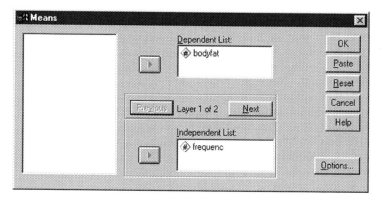

Compare Means/Independent-Samples T Test (Dialog box 63)

Use this test to examine the differences between two groups of participants (e.g., athletes from club A vs. athletes from club B) in one variable (e.g., take-off velocity in the long jump).

Table 17

Report

BODYFAT

FREQUENC	GENDER	Mean	Std. Deviation	N
sometimes	males	12.78	3.19	10
	Total	12.78	3.19	10
very often	females	17.39	5.08	10
	Total	17.39	5.08	10
Total	males	12.78	3.19	10
	females	17.39	5.08	10
	Total	15.09	4.76	20

Assumptions

There are four main assumptions for this test (Vincent, 1999):

1. The data must be parametric, that is, they should be measured on an interval or ratio scale (see Chapter 1). If this is not the case, use a non-paramatetric equivalent test (see *Non parametric tests-2 independent samples* in the *Analyze* menu).

2. The samples should be randomly selected from the population, so that the results of the *t* test can be generalised from the sample to the population.

3. The two samples should come from populations which have approximately the same variance (i.e., homogeneity of variance assumption). Use the Levene test (see below) to test this assumption.

4. The scores of the dependent variable should come from a population which is normally distributed (i.e., normality assumption). This assumption could be tested using the *Q-Q plot* and the *normality* tests in the *Descriptive Statistics/Explore* option of the *Analyze* menu. In the same option, you can also ask for a *Boxplot* to identify possible outliers. You can also request a *Histogram with normal curve* in the *Descriptive Statistics/Frequencies* option of the same menu. Lastly, in the *Frequencies* option you can obtain the skewness and kurtosis values. If the ratio of *skewness* or *kurtosis* to their respective *standard errors* is above 1.96, the data are probably not normally distributed.

Bear in mind that the *t* test is fairly robust to moderate violations of the homogeneity of variance and normality assumptions. If there is a strong violation of the assumptions, consider using the non-parametric equivalent test.

How to carry out the test

In the example shown in Dialog box 63, move the dependent variable that will serve as a measure of comparison (i.e., *velocity*) into the *Test Variable(s)* box. If you want to perform more than one *t* test using different dependent variables, move all the dependent variables into this box.

The *grouping* (independent) *variable* is *club*. You should already have in the data file a variable called *club* which has assigned different codes to different clubs (e.g., code 1 to participants from club A and code 2 to participants from club B). Variable coding is essential; otherwise, you will not be able to carry out the *independent samples t test* (Figure 21).

If the *grouping variable* is continuous (e.g., strength, time), you need to dichotomise it by identifying a *Cut point*. This cut-off point could be the median value of the variable that will split the scores into 2 groups (see *Compute* in the *Transform* menu to compute a new categorical variable that will contain the codes for the two new groups). Click *Continue* and then *OK* (Dialog box 64).

Table 18 presents the sample size, mean, standard deviation, and standard error of the mean (i.e., amount of error in the prediction of the population mean) in each group. The statistical comparison of the group means is performed in Table 19. If the Levene test is significant, you should conclude that the variances of the take-off velocity scores in the two groups are not homogeneous. In this case, you should report the *t* value that corresponds to the *equal variances not assumed*. If the Levene test is not significant, you should conclude that the variances are homogeneous and you should report the *t* value that corresponds to the *equal variances assumed*.[1]

The Levene test in Table 18 is not significant ($F = .81$; $p = .38$, which is greater than .05), and the corresponding *t* value is significant ($t = 9.96$; $p = .000$). Therefore, you should conclude that the mean scores of take-off velocity differ

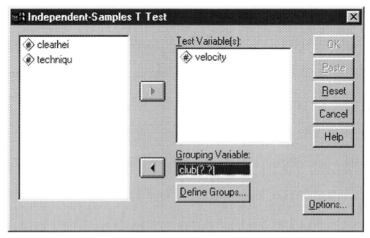

Dialog box 63

[1] In Table 19 both tests give the same result, but this is not always the case.

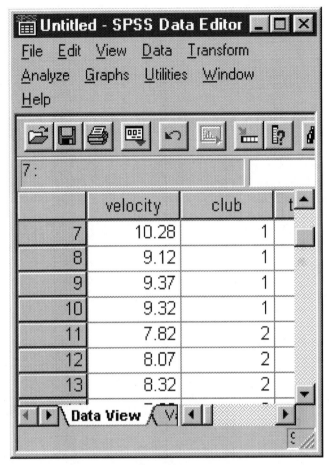

Figure 21

Dialog box 64

significantly between the two groups. As you can see, long jumpers from club A have significantly higher velocity than those from Club B ($M = 9.63$ compared to $M = 7.50$). Table 19 shows that the mean difference between the two groups is 2.13. The *Lower* and *Upper* values represent scores which are two standard errors below and above the mean difference respectively (i.e., *95% confidence interval*).

Table 18

Group Statistics

	CLUB	N	Mean	Std. Deviation	Std. Error Mean
VELOCITY	Group A	10	9.6320	.5248	.1659
	Group B	10	7.4950	.4291	.1357

Sometimes, the sign of the *t* value is negative. This does not mean that your analysis is wrong. It simply signifies that the mean of the second group is higher than the mean of the first group. In Table 19, the *t* value was positive because the first group had a higher mean than the second group.

In the various statistical texts you will frequently come across the terms 'one-tailed' and 'two-tailed' *t* tests. The one-tailed test is used when two groups are expected to differ in a particular direction. For example, elite athletes are predicted to have <u>higher</u> take-off velocity compared to non-elite ones. In other cases, such as the one presented here, you may not have a clear hypothesis regarding the direction of the difference. Therefore, you need to use a two-tailed *t* test. SPSS provides the two-tailed significance values only. To obtain the one-tailed significance values you need to consult a table of critical *t* values which is located at the end of most statistical texts.

How to report the test
When you present the results of a *t* test you need to report the means and standard deviations of the two groups (club A/club B), the Levene test and its significance level, as well as the *t* value, its degrees of freedom (*df*), and significance level. Example 1 shows how you could report the results of a *t* test in a table.

Example 1: Differences in take-off velocity between long-jumpers from Clubs A and B

	M (SD)	t	df
Take-off velocity of high jumpers fom Club A	9.63 (.52)	9.96**	18
Take-off velocity of high jumpers fom Club B	7.49 (.43)		

** *p* <.01

Compare Means/Paired-Samples T Test

This is also a *t* test, but it should be used when one group of people is measured *twice* on the same variable. This test is appropriate for pre-test/post-test designs. In contrast, the *Independent Samples T Test* compares two groups of people at one point in time. The data for *Paired-Samples T Test* must be parametric, that

Table 19

Independent Samples Test

		Levene's Test for Equality of Variances		t-test for Equality of Means						
									95% Confidence Interval of the Difference	
		F	Sig.	t	df	Sig. (2-tailed)	Mean Difference	Std. Error Difference	Lower	Upper
SPEED	Equal variances assumed	.814	.379	9.969	18	.000	2.1370	.2144	1.6866	2.5874
	Equal variances not assumed			9.969	17.318	.000	2.1370	.2144	1.6854	2.5886

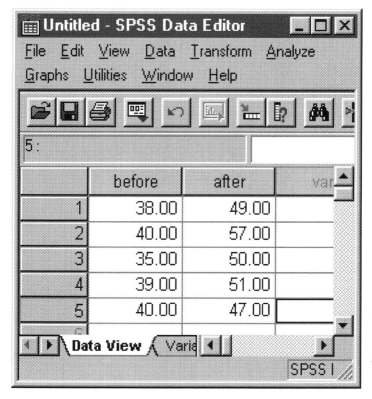

Figure 22

is, they should be measured on an interval or ratio scale (see Chapter 1). If this is not the case, use a non-parametric equivalent test (see *Non parametric tests-2 related samples* in the *Analyze* menu). The assumptions of the *Independent Samples T Test* apply to this test as well.

An example of a paired samples *t* test is a study in which you compare the aerobic capacity of one group of participants *before* and *after* a 10-week training programme (Figure 22). The two aerobic capacity measures should be moved into the *Paired Variables* box (you can perform more than one *t* test with different variables by inserting all the appropriate pairs in this box). Then click *OK* (Dialog box 65).

Table 20 shows that there has been an improvement in aerobic capacity. The negative sign of the *t* value (-7.207) indicates that the mean aerobic capacity after the programme is higher than the mean aerobic capacity before the start of the programme. The *t* value is significant ($p = .002$). Therefore, you should conclude that the mean scores before and after the training programme differ significantly, in that the aerobic capacity of the participants has improved significantly over the 10 weeks. The *Lower* and *Upper* values represent scores which are two standard errors below and above the mean difference respectively

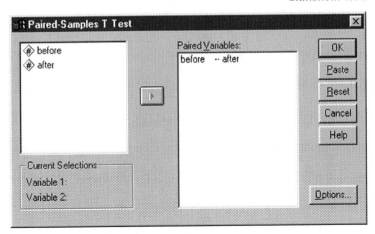

Dialog box 65

(i.e., *95% confidence interval*). Table 21 presents the descriptive statistics before and after the training programme.

Although it may sound confusing, this test can also be used for two different groups of people who are matched on one or more characteristics (e.g., age), and thus they are no longer independent. Be aware that when using *Independent-Samples T Test* groups are not matched on any variables as it is assumed that they have been randomly selected from the population. For an extensive discussion of matched pairs, see Vincent (1999).

How to report the test
When you present the results of a paired samples *t* test you need to report the mean scores and the standard deviations of the dependent variable (aerobic capacity) in the two conditions (pre-test/post-test), the *t* value, its degrees of freedom (*df*) and significance level. Example 2 shows how you could report the results of a *t* test in a table.

Example 2: Improvements in aerobic capacity after a ten-week training programme

	M (SD)	t	df
Pre-test aerobic capacity	38.40 (2.07)	-7.21^{**}	4
Post-test aerobic capacity	50.80 (3.77)		

$^{**}p < .05$

Compare Means/One-Way ANOVA

This test is an extension of the Independent Samples *T Test*. It is used when an independent variable (e.g., clearance height in high jump) has more than two

Table 20

Paired Samples Test

		Paired Differences						
					95% Confidence Interval of the Difference			
	Mean	Std. Deviation	Std. Error Mean	Lower	Upper	t	df	Sig. (2-tailed)
Pair 1 BEFORE - AFTER	-12.4000	3.8471	1.7205	-17.1768	-7.6232	-7.207	4	.002

Table 21

Paired Samples Statistics

		Mean	N	Std. Deviation	Std. Error Mean
Pair 1	BEFORE	38.4000	5	2.0736	.9274
	AFTER	50.8000	5	3.7683	1.6852

groups (e.g., the Western Roll, Straddle, and Fosbury styles). One could argue that three *t* tests (i.e., Western Roll vs. Straddle, Western Roll vs. Fosbury, and Straddle vs. Fosbury) could be used to compare the different styles. However, statisticians (e.g., Tabachnick and Fidell, 1996) tell us that multiple comparisons can increase the probability of at least one test being significant when in fact it is not (i.e., Type I error). That is, multiple *t* tests can increase the significance level above the acceptable value of 0.05. To deal with this problem, it is preferable to conduct an Analysis of Variance (ANOVA) than multiple *t* tests. When there is one independent variable with three or more levels (e.g., high jump styles) then the analysis is called one-way ANOVA. When there are two or more independent variables (e.g., high jump styles and years of training) then the analysis is called factorial ANOVA. Note that in both one-way ANOVA and factorial ANOVA there is only one dependent variable. If you have two or more dependent variables you need either to perform separate ANOVA tests for each dependent variable or use Multivariate Analysis of Variance (MANOVA; see *General Linear Model/Multivariate* in the *Analyze* menu). For a detailed discussion of the advantages and disadvantages of MANOVA compared to ANOVA, see Vincent (1999).

Assumptions
ANOVA tests are based on the following assumptions (Vincent, 1999):

1. The data should be parametric, measured on an interval or ratio scale. For ordinal data use a non-parametric equivalent test (see *Non-parametric tests-K independent samples* in the *Analyze* menu).
2. Independence. There should be no relationship between the scores of the dependent variable in the different groups. If the scores are related (e.g., the groups represent different conditions under which a participant has been repeatedly measured), consider using the *Repeated Measures* ANOVA test (see below).
3. Homogeneity of variances. The groups should come from populations which have equal or nearly equal variances in the scores of the dependent variable. Use the Levene test (see *Options* below) to check this assumption. You can also look at the spread of the scores in a box plot (*Factor levels together*) produced with the *Descriptive Statistics/Explore* option of the

Analyze menu. According to Vincent (1999), ANOVA is relatively robust to violations of this assumption provided that the largest group variance is not more than two times greater than the smallest group variance.

4. Normality. The scores of the dependent variables in each group should come from populations which are normally distributed. To assess normality in each group, use the procedures outlined in the *Independent-Samples T Test* (see above). Note that ANOVA is not heavily dependent on the assumption of normality.

If you suspect serious violations of the ANOVA assumptions, consider using a non-parametric equivalent test. Alternatively, you can transform the dependent variable so that it is more normal or the variances in the group are more similar. Data transformations are beyond the scope of this book. Experienced SPPS users can use one of the *Functions* in the *Compute Variable* option of the *Transform* menu.

How to carry out the test

In the example shown in Figure 23, suppose you want to examine differences in clearance height between three groups of high jumpers who use one of the three styles. Clearance height is the difference between the maximum height reached by the centre of gravity and the height of the crossbar. Note that in this example there is ONE Independent variable (style) which has three levels.

It is worth noting that you do not need to specify the levels of the independent variable in Dialog box 66, as it is the case when performing an independent samples *t* test. However, you still need to have a variable in the data file which will contain the codes for the different styles. Variable coding is essential; otherwise, you will not be able to carry out the ANOVA test (see *Compute* in the *Transform* menu to create a new categorical variable with the codes for the different groups).

Move clearance height into the *Dependent List* box. Note that you can perform multiple one-way ANOVA tests by moving all the dependent variables into that box. ANOVA results will tell you whether there is a significant difference between the three groups on the dependent variable, but they will not tell you where the difference lies, for example, whether the clearance height will differ between high jumpers who use the Western Roll and the Fosbury style, or between those who use the Straddle and the Fosbury style. To find out where the differences lie, click on *Post Hoc* (Dialog box 67).

When *equal variances are assumed*, or preferably found using the Levene test (see *Options* below), choose the *Tukey* or the *Scheffe* test, or any other test recommended in statistical texts. To alter the significance level for the mean comparisons and prevent Type I error, type a new value in the *Significance level* box. Click *Continue*. The *Options* in Dialog box 66 can be used to ask for descriptive statistics and to carry out the Levene test (*Homogeneity of variance*). You can also request a *Means plot* which will present the mean scores of each style on the dependent variable. Click *OK*.

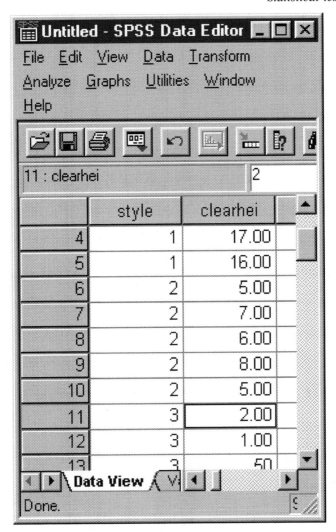

Figure 23

The results show that the ANOVA test is significant (F (2, 12) = 111.13; $p = .000$) (Table 22). This indicates that the three styles differ significantly in clearance height. *Sum of squares* represents the sums of squared differences between individual scores and their means. *Mean square* indicates the ratio of sum of squares to the degrees of freedom.

Table 23 shows the descriptive statistics for the three styles. The *Lower Bound* and *Upper Bound* values represent scores which are two standard deviations below and above the mean scores respectively (i.e., *95% confidence interval*).

The ANOVA test is significant, but you still need to find out which style differs from the others. Note that if the F value was not significant, you should

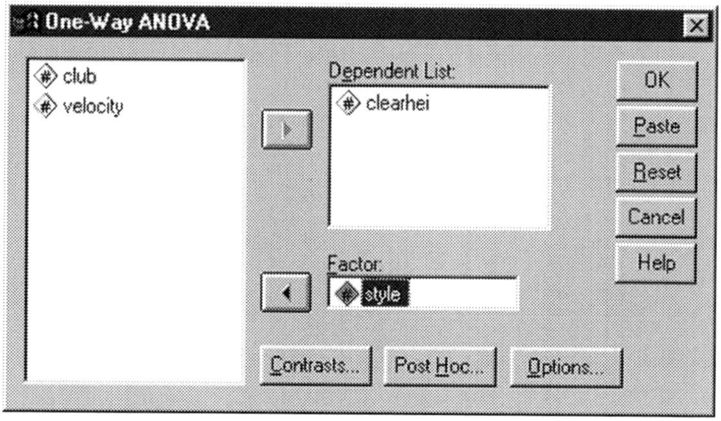

Dialog box 66

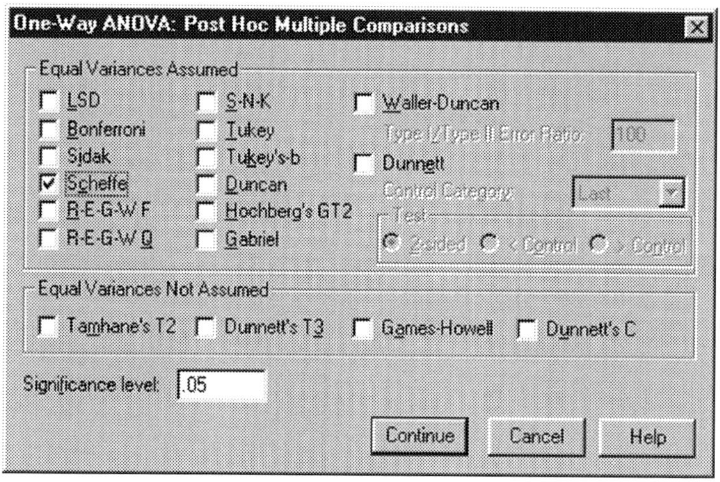

Dialog box 67

Table 22

ANOVA

CLEARHEI

	Sum of Squares	df	Mean Square	F	Sig.
Between Groups	481.045	2	240.523	111.130	.000
Within Groups	25.972	12	2.164		
Total	507.017	14			

Table 23

Descriptives

CLEARHEI

| | N | Mean | Std. Deviation | Std. Error | 95% Confidence Interval for Mean | | Minimum | Maximum |
					Lower Bound	Upper Bound		
Western Roll	5	14.6000	2.0736	.9274	12.0252	17.1748	12.00	17.00
Straddle	5	6.2000	1.3038	.5831	4.5811	7.8189	5.00	8.00
Fosbury	5	.8400	.7021	.3140	-3.1821E-02	1.7118	.30	2.00
Total	15	7.2133	6.0179	1.5538	3.8807	10.5460	.30	17.00

have stopped here and reported that the three styles did not differ significantly in clearance height.

The *post-hoc* Tukey test compares the clearance height of the three styles. Note that the use of the Tukey test is justified because the Levene Test was not significant (the actual value of the test is not shown here). If the Levene Test was significant, you should have used one of the *post-hoc* tests under the *equal variances not assumed* section of Dialog box 67. Table 24 shows that the clearance height differs significantly among all three styles. For example, when using the Fosbury style the clearance height is 13.76 cm and 5.36 cm smaller than the clearance height obtained with the Western Roll and the Straddle styles respectively. Table 24 shows the mean difference in clearance height, as well its standard error, significance level and 95% confidence intervals. These intervals show the values two standard errors below (*Lower Bound*) and above (*Upper Bound*) the mean difference respectively.

Note that some statisticians (e.g., Pedhazur and Schmelkin, 1991) do not recommend the use of *post-hoc* tests, because these tests require a large number of mean comparisons which can increase the probability for Type I error (especially if the significance level in Dialog box 67 is not adjusted). Pedhazur and Schmelkin (1991) advocate the use of *a priori* planned comparisons to prevent Type I errors. *A priori* comparisons perform only a limited number of comparisons between mean scores, because they are based on a theory that specifies which comparisons are important and which are not. For example, the *post-hoc* Tukey test above carried out three mean comparisons contrasting each style with the others. If there were five styles, you would have performed 10 different mean comparisons. However, with *a priori* planned comparisons you could limit the comparisons to a certain number specified by a theory or previous research (e.g., compare the Straddle and Fosbury styles only).

To carry out *a priori* planned comparisons, click *Contrasts* in Dialog box 66 to open Dialog box 68. Select *Polynomial* and *Linear* under the *Degree* option. Each style should be given a comparison coefficient. The order of the coefficients is crucial because each coefficient corresponds to a different high jump style. Although there are many types of planned comparisons, orthogonal ones are most often used. Orthogonal planned comparisons require that the sum of the coefficients is zero in any given comparison. That is, if you want to compare the first and the third style, you should assign coefficient 1 to the first style (Western Roll), coefficient 0 to the second style (Straddle), and coefficient -1 to the third style (Fosbury) (i.e., $1 + 0 - 1 = 0$). If the first style was compared with the other two styles, the coefficients for the three styles should have been -2, 1, and 1 respectively. Use the *Add* button to add each coefficient. For more complicated designs use the *Next* button to add another set of contrasts. Click *Continue* and when you get back to Dialog box 66 click *OK*. The output tables (Tables 25, 26) list the contrast coefficients and the results of the planned comparisons between the first and the third style. As you can see, the *t* test is significant which indicates that the difference in clearance height between the

Table 24

Multiple Comparisons

Dependent Variable: CLEARHEI

Scheffe

(I) STYLE	(J) STYLE	Mean Difference (I-J)	Std. Error	Sig.	95% Confidence Interval	
					Lower Bound	Upper Bound
Western Roll	Straddle	8.4000*	.9304	.000	5.8063	10.9937
	Fosbury	13.7600*	.9304	.000	11.1663	16.3537
Straddle	Western Roll	-8.4000*	.9304	.000	-10.9937	-5.8063
	Fosbury	5.3600*	.9304	.000	2.7663	7.9537
Fosbury	Western Roll	-13.7600*	.9304	.000	-16.3537	-11.1663
	Straddle	-5.3600*	.9304	.000	-7.9537	-2.7663

*. The mean difference is significant at the .05 level.

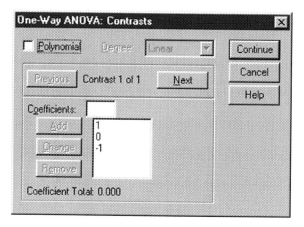

Dialog box 68

Table 25

Contrast Coefficients

Contrast	STYLE		
	Western Roll	Straddle	Fosbury
1	-1	0	1

Western Roll and the Fosbury styles is significant. Table 26 also shows the mean difference between the two styles (*Value of Contrast*) and the standard error of the difference.

How to report the test

When you present the results of one-way ANOVA tests you should report the mean and standard deviation scores of the different groups on the dependent variable, the *F* value, the between groups and within groups degrees of freedom, and the significance level of the *F* value. If the *F* value is significant, you should also report which groups differ from the others based on the results of the *post-hoc* tests or the planned comparisons. Example 3 shows how you could report the results of one-way ANOVA tests in a table:

Table 26

Contrast Tests

	Contrast	Value of Contrast	Std. Error	t	df	Sig. (2-tailed)
CLEARHEI Assume equal variances	1	-13.7600	.9304	-14.789	12	.000
Does not assume equal	1	-13.7600	.9791	-14.054	4.905	.000

Example 3: Differences in clearance height among three different high jump styles

	M (SD)	t	df
Western Roll	14.60 (2.07)	111.13*	2, 12
Straddle	6.20 (1.30)		
Fosbiry	.84 (.70)		

** *p* < .01

General Linear Model/Univariate

This is an extension of one-way ANOVA and it is used when you have two or more independent variables. This analysis is also called factorial ANOVA. Usually, up to three-way ANOVA tests (three independent variables or factors) are reported in the literature, although it is possible to examine more than three factors. The term *Univariate* means that there is only one dependent variable, in contrast to *Multivariate* (see below), which indicates the testing of several dependent variables.

Assumptions

The assumptions of factorial ANOVA are similar to those required for one-way ANOVA and can be tested in the same way. In addition, *Univariate* offers *spread vs. level plots* and *residual plots* (see below) which can be used to examine the assumption of homogeneity of variances. Residuals represent, for each case, the difference between the actual value of the dependent variable minus the value predicted by the independent variables. Furthermore, the *Save* option (see below) saves in the data file the residuals (*unstandardized, standardized, studentized, deleted*) of the analysis which can be analysed in order to examine further the assumptions of ANOVA. Nevill (2000) and Norusis (1998) have described a number of ways which can be used to analyse residuals. In essence, if the assumptions of the ANOVA tests are met, the residuals should have the following characteristics:

1. Residuals should be normally distributed. You can assess the normality of residuals using exactly the same procedures you would use with ordinary variables (for a detailed discussion, see assumption 4 in the *Independent-Samples T Test*). In some cases, the normality assumption is not met because the distribution of the residuals is asymmetrical, or because it reveals the presence of several outliers. In Figure 24 the residuals tends to cluster around the straight line, thus indicating normality. Absence of normality is evident when the residuals deviate from the straight line by curving above or below it.

2. Residuals should have the same variance for all values of the independent variables (homoscedasticity assumption). To test this assumption, you can plot a *simple scatterplot* (see Graphs menu) showing the *studentized*

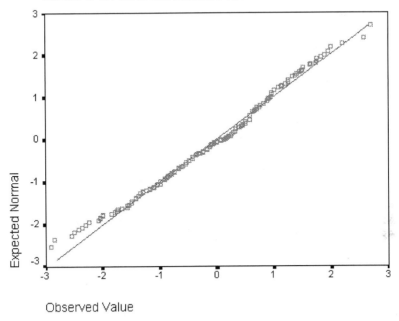

Figure 24

residuals against the *predicted values* (to save these values in the data file, use the *Save* option below). If this assumption is met, there should be no specific pattern in the spread of the residuals. However, in Figure 25, there seems to be a pattern as the variability of the residuals decreases with increasing predicted values (i.e., heteroscedasticity). Usually, the literature reports cases where the variability of the residuals increases at larger predicted values. An alternative way to test this assumption is to re-run the *Univariate* analysis using the residuals as the dependent variable. A non-significant Levene test will signify that the assumption of homogeneous variances cannot be rejected. Heteroscedasticity reduces the power of ANOVA to discover significant results (i.e., Type II error).

3. The relationship between the residuals and the predicted values of the dependent variable should be linear. However, inspection of Figure 25 reveals that this relationship is non-linear. Non-linearity also reduces the power of ANOVA.

4. The residuals are independent. This assumption requires that the score of one participant is not related in any way to the score of another participant. This assumption is violated when the order in which participants are assessed may influence their performance. For example, imagine an inexperienced researcher who is able to provide better instructions to the participants who join his/her experiment later on rather than earlier. Better

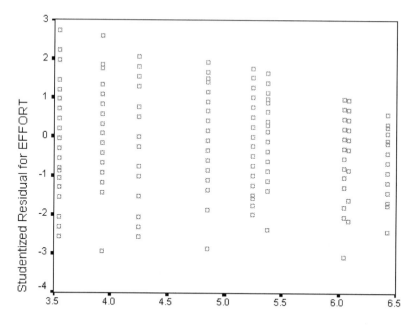

Figure 25

instructions may help these participants to perform better. Figure 26 shows that there is no evident relationship between the residuals and the order in which the dependent measure was taken.

If some of these assumptions are violated, you may have to transform the dependent variable. However, bear in mind that the F value is relatively robust to such violations, provided that the sample sizes in the groups of the independent variables are relatively equal.

How to carry out the test
Suppose you want to look at differences in self-reported effort (dependent variable) in a physical education class. Factorial ANOVA will examine differences in effort among different levels (1 = little, 2 = moderate, 3 = high) of enjoyment of physical education and support that pupils receive from their PE teachers. Note that you need to have two variables in the data file which contain the codes for the different levels (Figure 27). Variable coding is essential to carry out the factorial ANOVA test (see *Compute* in the *Transform* menu to create a new categorical variable with the codes for the different groups).

The effects of enjoyment and support are called main effects. Factorial ANOVA will also test for interaction effects, that is, whether there is a combined

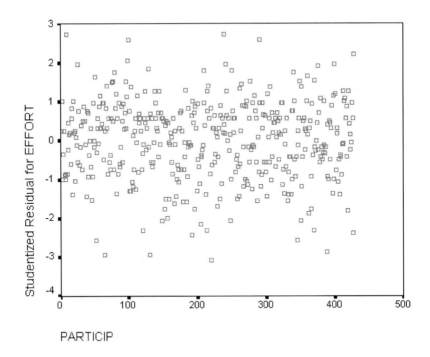

PARTICIP

Figure 26

effect of enjoyment and support on effort. An example of significant interaction is when the same levels of support predict different levels of effort depending on the amount of enjoyment. If there is no significant interaction, different levels of enjoyment will not influence the effect of support on effort (as in Figure 30).

Move *effort* into the *Dependent Variable* box. Remember that ANOVA tests have only one dependent variable. Move the independent variables *enjoymen* and *support* into the *Fixed Factor(s)* box. If you want to carry out an ANCOVA, that is an Analysis of Covariance, move one or more covariates into the *Covariate(s)* box. Covariates are confounding variables which can have an undue effect on the results of ANOVA tests. By identifying covariates, researchers try to control (factor out) their influence. For example, one may argue that different levels of competence may have a confounding effect. Often, those who feel more competent in PE are the ones who try harder because they know they will be successful. By identifying competence as a covariate, you will be able to answer the question of what the effects of enjoyment and support on effort are, after adjusting differences in levels of competence.

Click on *Options* in Dialog box 69. To estimate the mean scores on effort for the different levels of enjoyment and support, move these variables and their interaction into the *Display Means for* box in Dialog box 70. Under *Display* you can select a number of options depending on your research questions and your experience with statistics. It would be useful to ask for *descriptive statistics*

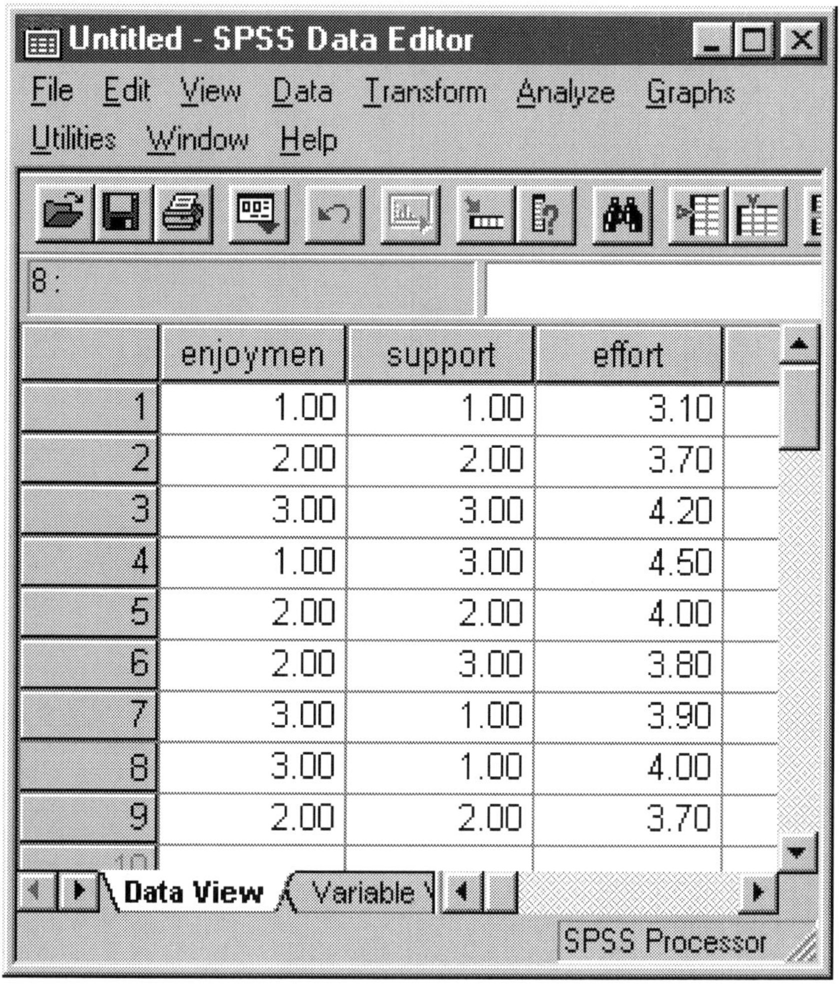

Figure 27

(means, standard deviations and counts), and *estimates of effect size* (eta squared; η^2) which indicate the amount of variance in the dependent variable explained by an independent variable. The eta squared varies between 0.00 and 1 with higher values indicating better prediction of the dependent variable. Select *Observed Power* to estimate the probability that the analysis will detect differences between groups. Increased power reduces Type II error. Also, select *homogeneity tests* (i.e., Levene tests) to examine the homogeneity of variances assumption of the ANOVA test. This assumption requires that the variance of the dependent variable is equal across all combinations of the independent variables. *Spread vs. level plot* and the *Residual plot* can also be used to examine the assumption of homogeneity of variances. *Spread vs. level plot* produces two plots of observed group means against standard deviations and variances.

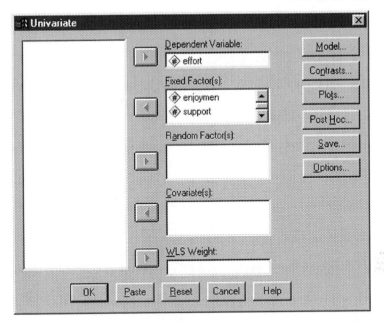

Dialog box 69

Residual plot produces a *matrix scatterplot* of the observed against the predicted and standardised residuals. If the homogeneity assumption is satisfied, the plots should not show any systematic effect, such as a linear relationship between means and variances, or non-random patterns in the residual plots. In the *Significance level* box at the bottom of Dialog box 70 you can decrease the level of significance used in the *post-hoc* comparisons to prevent Type I error (see the relevant discussion in *One-way ANOVA* of the *Analyze* menu). Click *Continue*.

The *Save* option of Dialog box 69 creates new variables in the data file (Dialog box 71). Under *Predicted Values*, you can create a variable showing, for each case, the *Unstandardized* predicted value of the dependent variable. You can also request the *Standard error* of the *Predicted values*. The two measures under *Diagnostics* (*Cook's distance* and *Leverage value*) show the degree to which residuals would change if a particular case was deleted. It is wise to delete cases with large values on any of the *Diagnostics* measures. Lastly, under *Residuals* you can save in the data file the *Unstandardized* and *Standardized residuals* (i.e., differences between the actual values of the dependent variable and those predicted by the independent variables). You can also save the *Studentized residuals* which represent the ratio of *Unstandardized residual* to an estimate of the standard deviation of the residual of a particular case. *Studentized residuals* have the advantage of taking into account differences in variability from case to case. Lastly, *Deleted residuals* represent the *Studentized residuals* of a particular case when this case has been excluded from the analysis (Norusis, 1998).

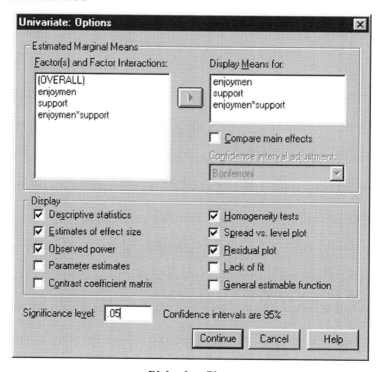

Dialog box 70

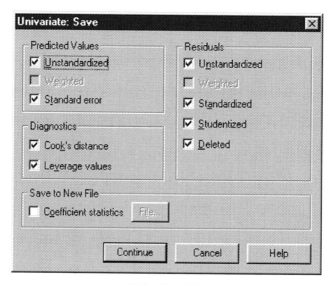

Dialog box 71

Dialog box 72

Click *Post Hoc* in Dialog box 69. ANOVA results will tell you whether the different levels (little, moderate, high) of the independent variables differ in the dependent variable, but they will not tell you where the difference lies. For example, the ANOVA results may tell you that the three levels of enjoyment differ in their mean scores on effort. However, you need to know whether, for example, the high enjoyment group exerts more effort than the moderate or the low enjoyment groups. To find out where the differences among the observed means lie, click on *Post Hoc* to open Dialog box 72. When *equal variances are assumed*, or preferably found with a non-significant Levene test (see *Homogeneity tests* in Dialog box 70), the *Scheffe* or *Tukey* test should be used. Click *Continue*.

Click *Plots* in Dialog box 69. Profile plots are useful when you want to draw the interaction between the independent factors. Move the two independent factors into the *Horizontal Axis* and *Separate Lines* boxes (try swapping the factors in the two boxes to create the most easily interpretable plot). At the bottom of Dialog box 73, click *Add* to request the interaction plot. Parallel or near parallel lines in the plot indicate that there is no interaction between the independent factors. Intersecting lines usually indicate a significant interaction. When you finish, click *Continue*.

The *Contrasts* option of Dialog box 69 allows advanced SPSS users to test for differences among the levels of an independent variable. *Model* in Dialog box 69 allows you to create complicated factorial designs (Dialog box 74). Usually, a *Full factorial* model is chosen that examines all main and interaction effects. However, you can build up your own *Custom* model by specifying, for example, that you want to examine main effects only. In that case, move the two

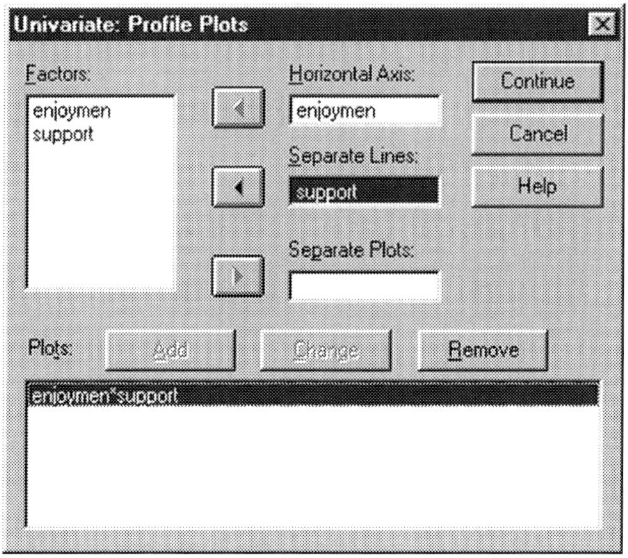

Dialog box 73

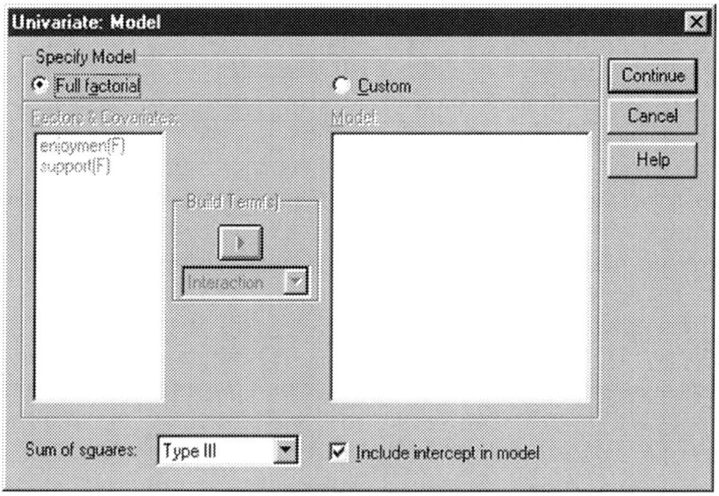

Dialog box 74

independent factors in the *Model* box and select *Main effects* from the *Build Terms* menu. Click *Continue* to get back to Dialog box 69 and then click *OK*.

Part of the output is displayed in Figure 28. The *Spread vs. Level Plot* shows the means versus the variances for each of the nine possible combinations among the groups of the independent variables. It seems that the variability in the scores decreases as the mean increases.

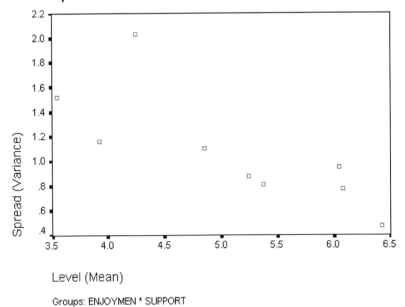

Figure 28

The *Residual plot* shows that the residuals are not random. As you can see at the top centre of the plot, there is a pattern of decreased variability between observed and predicted residuals as the values increase (Figure 29). Taken together, Figures 28 and 29 indicate that the homogeneity assumption is not satisfied. One way of dealing with this problem is to transform the dependent variable in order to achieve homogeneity. Alternatively, you can go back and create different groups of almost equal size. ANOVA tests are not affected too much by violations of the homogeneity assumption as long as the group sizes are almost equal.

The *eta squared* value for enjoyment (η^2) shows that this variable explains around 36% of the variance in effort scores. The power of the two main effects is large, whereas the power of the interaction effect is very small. The F values for *support* and *enjoyment* are significant. The interaction effect of support and enjoyment has a non-significant F value. Therefore, there are two significant main effects but no significant interaction effect (Table 27).

An inspection of the mean scores shows that as the levels of enjoyment and support increase, so does the level of effort in PE classes (Tables 28 and 29).

The ANOVA tests showed that the three enjoyment and support groups differ in effort. However, you need to find out which group differs from the others. Note that if one of the main effects was not significant (e.g., enjoyment), you should have stopped here and reported that the three enjoyment groups did not

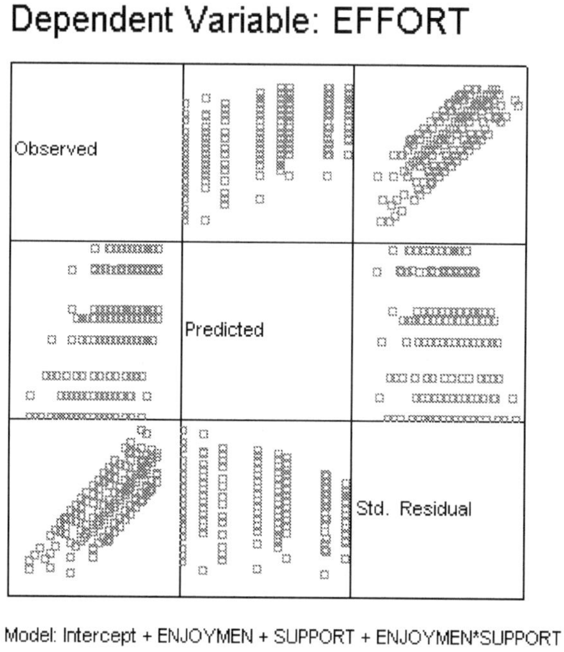

Dependent Variable: EFFORT

Model: Intercept + ENJOYMEN + SUPPORT + ENJOYMEN*SUPPORT

Figure 29

differ in self-reported effort. To examine where the significant differences lie, you need to look at the results of the *post-hoc* test. As the results in Tables 30 and 31 show, there are significant differences in effort among all three levels of support and enjoyment. For example, those who received high levels of support (*very much so*) were 1.31 points higher on effort compared to those who received little or no support, and 0.71 points higher compared to those who received a moderate amount of support.

Figure 30 verifies that the interaction between the two independent factors is not significant.

The ANCOVA output is very much the same. The main and interactive effects of the independent variables are adjusted by the covariate. Also, the mean scores (not shown here) of the different groups of the independent variables are adjusted by the covariate. In Figure 30, it is assumed that the covariate is competence. As you can see, competence has a significant main effect. Notice that the main effects of the independent variables remain significant after the adjustment (Table 32).

Assumptions

The assumptions of ANOVA tests are also applicable to ANCOVA tests. In addition, ANCOVA assumes that (Tabachnick and Fidell, 1996; Vincent, 1999):

Table 27

Tests of Between-Subjects Effects

Dependent Variable: EFFORT

Source	Type III Sum of Squares	df	Mean Square	F	Sig.	Eta Squared	Noncent. Parameter	Observed Power[a]
Corrected Model	381.967[b]	8	47.746	47.491	.000	.477	379.927	1.000
Intercept	8265.777	1	8265.777	8221.630	.000	.952	8221.630	1.000
ENJOYMEN	237.677	2	118.838	118.204	.000	.362	236.408	1.000
SUPPORT	12.537	2	6.269	6.235	.002	.029	12.470	.893
ENJOYMEN * SUPPORT	2.150	4	.537	.535	.710	.005	2.139	.180
Error	419.239	417	1.005					
Total	11658.875	426						
Corrected Total	801.206	425						

a. Computed using alpha = .05

b. R Squared = .477 (Adjusted R Squared = .467)

Table 28

---

1. ENJOYMEN

Dependent Variable: EFFORT

ENJOYMEN	Mean	Std. Error	95% Confidence Interval	
			Lower Bound	Upper Bound
Little or not at all	3.907	.101	3.708	4.106
Moderately so	5.155	.078	5.002	5.308
Very much so	6.180	.109	5.965	6.395

Table 29

---

2. SUPPORT

Dependent Variable: EFFORT

SUPPORT	Mean	Std. Error	95% Confidence Interval	
			Lower Bound	Upper Bound
Little or not at all	4.826	.108	4.614	5.038
Moderately so	5.069	.079	4.913	5.225
Very much so	5.347	.102	5.147	5.547

1. If there are multiple covariates, they should not be highly correlated ($r > .90$) with each other in order to avoid computational problems.
2. Relationships between covariate(s) and dependent variables, as well as between different covariates should be linear (i.e., represented by a straight line). Non-linear relationships increase the chance for Type II error, that is, the possibility of finding erroneous non-significant results. To test this assumption, use the residual plots described in Figure 29. You can also produce *simple scatterplots* (see the *Graphs* menu), plotting the dependent variable against each covariate at each level of the independent variable (use *Select Cases* in the *Data* menu to select each level in turn).
3. There is no interaction between the independent variable(s) and the covariate(s). A significant interaction indicates that the relationship between the dependent variable and the covariate(s) varies across the different categories of the independent variable(s). To test the assumption of non-significant interaction click *Model* in Dialog box 69 and select *Custom* to open Dialog box 75. In the *Factors & Covariates* box you can see the two independent factors and the covariate. Click on one variable at a time and move it into the *Model* box. Then, highlight one of the independent variables and the covariate, and move the pair into the *Model* box. Repeat the same procedure with the second independent variable and the covariate. Finally, highlight both two independent variables and the covariate and

Table 30

Multiple Comparisons

Dependent Variable: EFFORT

Tukey HSD

(I) ENJOYMEN	(J) ENJOYMEN	Mean Difference (I-J)	Std. Error	Sig.	95% Confidence Interval	
					Lower Bound	Upper Bound
Little or not at all	Moderately so	-1.3768*	.1150	.000	-1.6464	-1.1072
	Very much so	-2.4412*	.1295	.000	-2.7447	-2.1377
Moderately so	Little or not at all	1.3768*	.1150	.000	1.1072	1.6464
	Very much so	-1.0644*	.1200	.000	-1.3458	-.7831
Very much so	Little or not at all	2.4412*	.1295	.000	2.1377	2.7447
	Moderately so	1.0644*	.1200	.000	.7831	1.3458

Based on observed means.

*. The mean difference is significant at the .05 level.

Table 31

Multiple Comparisons

Dependent Variable: EFFORT
Tukey HSD

(I) SUPPORT	(J) SUPPORT	Mean Difference (I-J)	Std. Error	Sig.	95% Confidence Interval	
					Lower Bound	Upper Bound
Little or not at all	Moderately so	-.6039*	.1194	.000	-.8837	-.3241
	Very much so	-1.3133*	.1294	.000	-1.6165	-1.0101
Moderately so	Little or not at all	.6039*	.1194	.000	.3241	.8837
	Very much so	-.7094*	.1155	.000	-.9802	-.4386
Very much so	Little or not at all	1.3133*	.1294	.000	1.0101	1.6165
	Moderately so	.7094*	.1155	.000	.4386	.9802

Based on observed means.

*. The mean difference is significant at the .05 level.

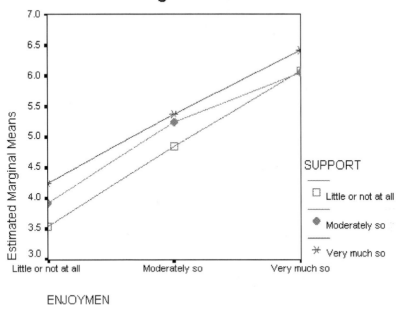

Figure 30

move all three into the *Model* box. The *custom* model you have created will test the interaction between the independent variables and the covariate. If none of these interactions is significant, you have a very good indication that the third assumption of the ANCOVA has been met. If there is strong evidence that the assumptions of ANCOVA have been violated, you may have to delete the specific covariate and use another variable.

How to report the test
When you present the results of factorial ANOVA you should report the mean scores of the different groups (little, moderate, very much support/enjoyment) on the dependent variable (effort). You should also report the *F* value of each main effect (support, enjoyment) and of the interaction effect (support x enjoyment), as well as the degrees of freedom and the significance level of each *F* value. If any of the *F* values is significant, you should describe which groups differ from the others based on the results of *post-hoc* tests. For ANCOVA, report in addition the effect of the covariate and the adjusted mean scores of the different groups. Example 4 shows how you could report the results of a factorial ANOVA in a table.

Results of an interaction test are best presented in a figure such as Figure 30.

Table 32

Tests of Between-Subjects Effects

Dependent Variable: EFFORT

Source	Type III Sum of Squares	df	Mean Square	F	Sig.	Eta Squared	Noncent. Parameter	Observed Power[a]
Corrected Model	482.512[b]	9	53.612	69.982	.000	.602	629.837	1.000
Intercept	109.347	1	109.347	142.734	.000	.255	142.734	1.000
COMPETEN	100.546	1	100.546	131.245	.000	.240	131.245	1.000
ENJOYMEN	33.494	2	16.747	21.861	.000	.095	43.721	1.000
SUPPORT	7.288	2	3.644	4.757	.009	.022	9.514	.792
ENJOYMEN * SUPPORT	1.872	4	.468	.611	.655	.006	2.444	.201
Error	318.694	416	.766					
Total	11658.875	426						
Corrected Total	801.206	425						

a. Computed using alpha = .05

b. R Squared = .602 (Adjusted R Squared = .594)

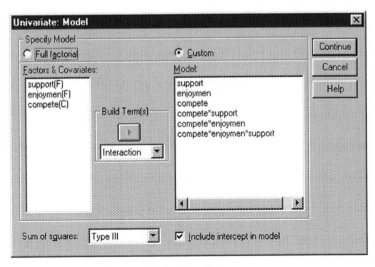

Dialog box 75

Example 4: Mean levels of effort in P.E. lessons among three groups which differ in enjoyment of P.E. and amount of support they receive from their P.E. teachers

	Effort				
	Group 1	Group 2	Group 3		
	M (SD)	M (SD)	M (SD)	F	df
Support	4.04$_a$ (.20)	4.72$_b$ (.14)	5.08$_c$ (.12)	9.86**	2,405
Enjoyment	4.01$_a$ (.20)	4.50$_a$ (.15)	5.35$_b$ (.12)	20.52**	2,405

$**p < .01$

Note: Group means sharing the same subscript ($_a$, $_b$ or $_c$) in the same row are not significantly different at the $p < .05$ level.

General Linear Model/Multivariate

This test is in many respects similar to *one-way ANOVA*. The difference is that *multivariate* tests analyse simultaneously more than one dependent variable. If no covariates are specified, the analysis is called MANOVA; otherwise it is named MANCOVA. Depending on the number of independent factors specified, the analysis can be named one-way MANOVA (MANCOVA), two-way MANOVA (MANCOVA), etc.

Assumptions

The assumptions required for MANOVA are similar to those required for one-way and factorial ANOVA, and can be tested in the same way. In addition,

MANOVA should satisfy the assumption of homogeneity of variance-covariance matrices, also called the sphericity assumption. This requires that variance-covariance matrices in each group are the same (i.e., come from the same population). To check this assumption, you can use the *Box's M* test provided with the *Homogeneity tests* (under *Options*). However, Tabachnick and Fidell (1996) argue that this test is very sensitive to minor violations of the assumption. In other words, this test is prone to show significant results, indicating violation of the sphericity assumption, even when such violation is minor. Therefore, Tabachnick and Fidell (1996) propose that if the group sizes are almost equal, the results of the *Box's M* test could be disregarded, as MANOVA will not be affected by violations of the sphericity assumption. In situations where the group sizes are unequal, try to randomly delete cases without substantially reducing the sample size. For further information about how to test this assumption, look at the *Classify Discriminant* option in the *Analyze* menu.

Tabachnick and Fidell (1996) identify a number of important issues associated with MANOVA. Firstly, in order to prevent Type II error, for each dependent variable there should be at least three participants in each group. A ratio smaller than 1:3 can lead to violation of the sphericity assumption. Secondly, Tabachnick and Fidell (1996) emphasise that MANOVA is particularly vulnerable to univariate and multivariate outliers. Univariate outliers are cases with extreme values on one variable, whereas multivariate outliers are cases with extreme values on a combination of variables. To identify multivariate outliers, you can use the *Mahalanobis distance* criterion described in the *Regression Linear* option of the *Analyze* menu. Lastly, the dependent variables should not be very highly correlated with each other. Very high correlations imply that some of the dependent variables provide redundant information and should, therefore, be removed.

How to carry out the test
Figure 31 examines whether high (code 1) and low (code 2) levels of somatic anxiety intensity (*somin*) and somatic anxiety interpretation or direction (*somadir*) differ in two dependent variables. These variables are the coping strategies of behavioural disengagement (*behadise*) and seeking of social support (*socisupp*). Note that the coding of the independent variables is essential to carry out the *multivariate* test (see *Compute* in the *Transform* menu to create codes for different groups).

All options in Dialog box 76 are similar to the ones described above for *univariate* analysis. A selected part of the output is shown in Table 33 which presents the multivariate effects of the independent variables. Multivariate effects indicate whether the combination of the dependent variables varies across the different levels of an independent variable. In this example, there are two independent variables, and therefore, there are two multivariate effects. There is also a third effect showing the interaction of the two variables. The main effect of somatic anxiety direction is significant, because the F value is significant (F (2, 348) = 7.088; p = 0.01). The main effect of somatic anxiety

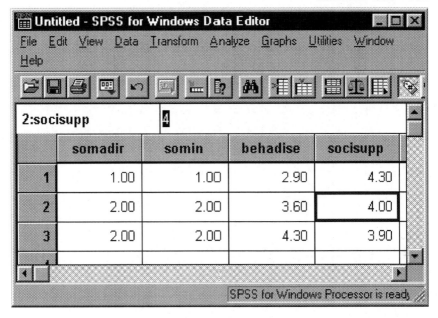

Figure 31

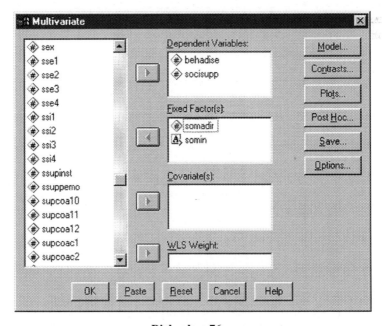

Dialog box 76

Table 33

Multivariate Tests[b]

Effect		Value	F	Hypothesis df	Error df	Sig.	Eta Squared
Intercept	Pillai's Trace	.883	1315.052[a]	2.000	348.000	.000	.883
	Wilks' Lambda	.117	1315.052[a]	2.000	348.000	.000	.883
	Hotelling's Trace	7.558	1315.052[a]	2.000	348.000	.000	.883
	Roy's Largest Root	7.558	1315.052[a]	2.000	348.000	.000	.883
SOMADIR	Pillai's Trace	.039	7.088[a]	2.000	348.000	.001	.039
	Wilks' Lambda	.961	7.088[a]	2.000	348.000	.001	.039
	Hotelling's Trace	.041	7.088[a]	2.000	348.000	.001	.039
	Roy's Largest Root	.041	7.088[a]	2.000	348.000	.001	.039
SOMIN	Pillai's Trace	.006	1.106[a]	2.000	348.000	.332	.006
	Wilks' Lambda	.994	1.106[a]	2.000	348.000	.332	.006
	Hotelling's Trace	.006	1.106[a]	2.000	348.000	.332	.006
	Roy's Largest Root	.006	1.106[a]	2.000	348.000	.332	.006
SOMADIR * SOMIN	Pillai's Trace	.027	4.783[a]	2.000	348.000	.009	.027
	Wilks' Lambda	.973	4.783[a]	2.000	348.000	.009	.027
	Hotelling's Trace	.027	4.783[a]	2.000	348.000	.009	.027
	Roy's Largest Root	.027	4.783[a]	2.000	348.000	.009	.027

a. Exact statistic

b. Design: Intercept+SOMADIR+SOMIN+SOMADIR * SOMIN

intensity is not significant, but the interaction between somatic anxiety intensity and somatic anxiety direction is significant.

You can now proceed and examine the univariate effects of each significant multivariate effect of Table 33. Whereas multivariate effects examine whether the combination of the dependent variables varies across the levels of an independent variable, univariate effects test whether a single dependent variable differs across the levels of an independent variable (Table 34).

The two levels of somatic anxiety direction (facilitative/debilitative) differ in behavioural disengagement $(F(1, 349) = 14.16; p = .00)$, but not in seeking social support $(F (1, 349) = .362; p= .55)$. Similarly, significant interaction effects are found in the use of behavioural disengagement, but not in seeking social support. Some statisticians (e.g., Pedhazur and Schmelkin, 1991) claim that in the presence of a significant interaction, main effects should be disregarded. This is because the independent variables act in combination and not in isolation (as the main effects imply) to predict the dependent variables. The interaction effect is shown in Figure 32. Similar high levels of somatic anxiety intensity predict significantly different levels of behavioural disengagement depending on whether somatic anxiety is perceived as debilitative (high use of disengagement) or facilitative (low use).

Note that if the interaction effect was not significant, you should have looked at the univariate main effect of somatic anxiety direction. The effect is significant $(F(1,349) = 14.15; p = .000)$ which means that facilitative and debilitative somatic anxiety differ in the use of the two coping strategies (look at the mean scores in the output to find out which variable has the highest mean). Owing to the fact that somatic anxiety has two levels (facilitative vs. debilitative), *post-hoc* tests are not performed as there is only one mean comparison to be made. If there were more than two levels, multiple comparisons should have been carried out using *post-hoc* tests.

As explained in the *Compare Means/One-Way ANOVA* option of the *Analyze* menu, some statisticians recommend the use of planned comparisons instead of *post-hoc* tests. Therefore, an alternative way to test for mean differences is to identify which are the significant univariate effects in MANOVA, and then carry out *one-way ANOVA* tests for each significant effect specifying *a priori* contrasts (see *Compare Means/One-Way ANOVA*). For example, suppose you have found a significant MANOVA effect when looking at the differences of four groups of sprinters in reaction time and movement time. Assume that subsequent univariate effects showed group differences in reaction time only. In view of these results, you can perform a *one-way ANOVA* test with the four groups as the independent variable and reaction time as the dependent variable, setting certain *a priori contrasts*.

How to report the test

When you present the results of MANOVA you should report the mean scores of the different groups (high and low anxiety intensity, facilitative and debilitative anxiety direction) on the dependent variables (social support and behavioural

Table 34

Source	Dependent Variable	Type III Sum of Squares	df	Mean Square	F	Sig.	Eta Squared
Corrected Model	BEHADISE	16.250[a]	3	5.417	11.199	.000	.088
	SOCISUPP	1.525[b]	3	.508	.492	.688	.004
Intercept	BEHADISE	566.076	1	566.076	1170.437	.000	.770
	SOCISUPP	1767.275	1	1767.275	1711.071	.000	.831
SOMADIR	BEHADISE	6.846	1	6.846	14.155	.000	.039
	SOCISUPP	.374	1	.374	.362	.548	.001
SOMIN	BEHADISE	.946	1	.946	1.956	.163	.006
	SOCISUPP	.148	1	.148	.143	.706	.000
SOMADIR × SOMIN	BEHADISE	4.449	1	4.449	9.199	.003	.026
	SOCISUPP	.858	1	.858	.831	.363	.002
Error	BEHADISE	168.792	349	.484			
	SOCISUPP	360.464	349	1.033			
Total	BEHADISE	850.257	353				
	SOCISUPP	2340.681	353				
Corrected Total	BEHADISE	185.042	352				
	SOCISUPP	361.989	352				

a. R Squared = .088 (Adjusted R Squared = .080)

b. R Squared = .004 (Adjusted R Squared = -.004)

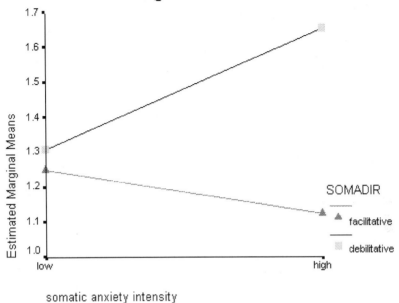

Figure 32

disengagement). For each main effect (anxiety intensity and direction) and for the interaction effect (intensity × direction) you should present the Wilk's lambda, the associated *F* value, the degrees of freedom and the significance level of the *F* value (see Table 33). If any of the multivariate *F* values is significant, you should proceed and report the univariate effects (*F* value, df, and significance level; see Table 34). If an independent variable has more than two groups you should mention the results of *post-hoc* tests or planned comparisons. Results of a MANOVA test can be reported in a table format similar to the one in Example 4.

General Linear Model/Repeated Measures

Pre-test/post-test designs have been described before in the *Compare means/ Paired Samples T Test* option of the *Analyze* menu. However, such designs look at changes in the scores of one dependent variable over two periods of time. With the *repeated measures* test you can examine more complicated designs.

Assumptions
All the assumptions described for ANOVA and MANOVA tests are also applicable to *repeated measures*. To analyse *repeated measures* you can take either a multivariate approach or a univariate approach (Nevill, 2000). The

univariate approach (repeated measures ANOVA) considers the repeated measures as levels of a within-subject factor. This approach requires that the data meet the assumption of sphericity, that is, the variance-covariance matrices in each measure should be equal (i.e., from the same population). The sphericity assumption protects you from making a Type I error. To test this assumption, use the *Mauchly's test of sphericity* (see below). If the test is significant, then the assumption has been violated. In such cases, you can use one of the three *epsilon correction* measures to adjust the degrees of freedom (for a more detailed discussion, see below). Alternatively, if the violation is severe, you can use the multivariate approach. Repeated MANOVA treats the repeated measures as multiple dependent variables. With this approach, the assumption of sphericity is not required. SPSS provides a table with multivariate tests which should be used only when the repeated MANOVA approach has been adopted. In the example below, the univariate approach was used because the data met the sphericity assumption.

How to carry out the test

Suppose you have three groups of participants with different *levels* of competitive experience (beginners = 1, intermediate = 2, advanced = 3) and you want to examine the number of errors they make in a complex motor skill under three conditions (low, moderate, and high anxiety). The three competitive experience levels represent the between-subjects variable and the three anxiety conditions the within-subjects variable, because all subjects are tested under all three anxiety conditions. Note that the *lownaxie, modanxie,* and *highanxi* variables represent the number of errors in each condition and not actual anxiety levels (Figure 33). Also, note that the between-subjects variable should be categorical (see *Compute* in the *Transform* menu to transform a continuous variable into a categorical).

Name the within-subject factor as *anxiety* (be careful, there should not be a variable with this name in the data file). In the *Number of Levels* box type 3, because there are 3 anxiety conditions. Click *Add*. Then click *Measure* to name your measure as *errors* (again, there should not be a variable with this name in the data file). Click *Add*. Repeat the above process if you have measured repeatedly more than one variable. Another variable you could have for example, measured across the three anxiety conditions is the heart rate of the participants. This model (which has not been used in the example here) involves more than one measure and is called a doubly multivariate repeated measures model. Finally click *Define* (Dialog box 77).

Move the three anxiety conditions into the *Within-Subjects Variables* box and the competitive level of the participants into the *Between-Subjects Factor(s)* box. The options at the bottom of Dialog box 78 have been described previously (see *General linear model/Univariate* in the *Analyze* menu). Finally, click *OK*.

Part of the output is presented in Tables 35 and 36. The descriptive statistics show that the low anxiety condition produces the least number of mistakes.

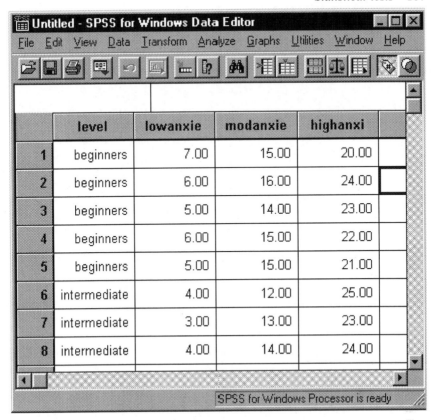

Figure 33

Also, in every condition advanced sport performers made fewer mistakes compared to the other two groups.

Table 37 shows the competitive level by anxiety condition breakdown of the number of errors. *Repeated measures* examine whether this interaction between *level* and *anxiety* is significant.

Before the results are explained, it is important to test the assumption of sphericity. The *Mauchly's* Test of Sphericity in Table 38 is not significant, and therefore, the sphericity assumption holds true in this sample. If the assumption was violated, you should have used one of the three *epsilon* corrections (*Greenhouse-Geisser, Huynh-Feldt*, or *Lower-bound*). Usually, the *Greenhouse-Geisser* correction is used in the literature. The *epsilon* corrections adjust (reduce) the degrees of freedom which are reported in Table 39, and thus make it more difficult to find significant *F* values. For example, in Table 39 the degrees of freedom for ANXIETY are 2, when sphericity is assumed. However, the degrees of freedom are decreased to 1.42 (2 x .714=1.42) when the *Greenhouse-Geisser* correction is applied. The univariate tests show that the within-subjects main effect is significant (*sphericity assumed*), but the interaction effect between *anxiety* and *level* is not significant.

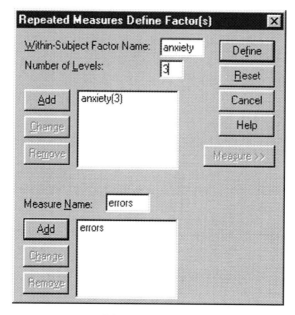

Dialog box 77

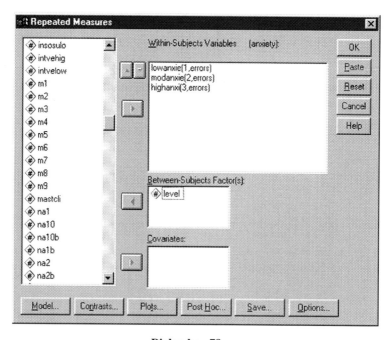

Dialog box 78

Table 35

2. ANXIETY

Measure: ERRORS

ANXIETY	Mean	Std. Error	95% Confidence Interval	
			Lower Bound	Upper Bound
1	3.933	.200	3.498	4.369
2	13.533	.309	12.860	14.207
3	21.533	.548	20.340	22.727

Table 36

1. LEVEL

Measure: ERRORS

LEVEL	Mean	Std. Error	95% Confidence Interval	
			Lower Bound	Upper Bound
beginners	14.267	.474	13.234	15.299
intermediate	12.867	.474	11.834	13.899
advanced	11.867	.474	10.834	12.899

Unfortunately, SPSS does not provide *post-hoc* tests to examine further the within-subject effects. That is, although you know that there is a significant difference in the number of errors across the three anxiety conditions, you do not know which condition differs significantly from the others. Does the high anxiety condition produce significantly more errors than the other two conditions, or does the difference lie between the high and the low anxiety conditions only? To answer such questions you need to calculate Tukey's *post-hoc* test using the formula presented by Vincent (1999).

Alternatively, you can carry out three paired samples *t* tests (see *Compare means/Paired Samples T Test* in the *Analyze* menu) comparing high and moderate anxiety, high and low, and moderate and low anxiety. For these multiple comparisons, the significance level should be adjusted by dividing the

Table 37

3. LEVEL * ANXIETY

Measure: ERRORS

LEVEL	ANXIETY	Mean	Std. Error	95% Confidence Interval	
				Lower Bound	Upper Bound
beginners	1	5.800	.346	5.045	6.555
	2	15.000	.535	13.833	16.167
	3	22.000	.949	19.933	24.067
intermediate	1	3.400	.346	2.645	4.155
	2	13.000	.535	11.833	14.167
	3	22.200	.949	20.133	24.267
advanced	1	2.600	.346	1.845	3.355
	2	12.600	.535	11.433	13.767
	3	20.400	.949	18.333	22.467

Table 38

Mauchly's Test of Sphericity[b]

Measure: ERRORS

Within Subjects Effect	Mauchly's W	Approx. Chi-Square	df	Sig.	Epsilon[a]		
					Greenhouse-Geisser	Huynh-Feldt	Lower-bound
ANXIETY	.599	5.642	2	.058	.714	.918	.500

Tests the null hypothesis that the error covariance matrix of the orthonormalized transformed dependent variab proportional to an identity matrix.

a. May be used to adjust the degrees of freedom for the averaged tests of significance. Corrected tests are displayed in the Tests of Within-Subjects Effects table.

b.
Design: Intercept+LEVEL
Within Subjects Design: ANXIETY

conventional 0.05 level with the number of t tests (i.e., 3). Therefore, the new significance level for the multiple comparisons should be $p = 0.017$. This is called the Bonferroni method of adjustment and is used in order to prevent Type I error.

The test for between-subjects effects (*Level*) is also significant. This indicates that there is a significant difference in the number of errors among the three competitive levels. Note that the term Error at the bottom of Table 40 refers to error variance in the ANOVA model and has nothing to do with the number of errors or mistakes in the complex motor skill.

Table 39

Tests of Within-Subjects Effects

Measure: ERRORS

Source		Type III Sum of Squares	df	Mean Square	F	Sig.
ANXIETY	Sphericity Assumed	2329.600	2	1164.800	735.663	.000
	Greenhouse-Geisser	2329.600	1.427	1632.183	735.663	.000
	Huynh-Feldt	2329.600	1.836	1268.984	735.663	.000
	Lower-bound	2329.600	1.000	2329.600	735.663	.000
ANXIETY * LEVEL	Sphericity Assumed	10.400	4	2.600	1.642	.196
	Greenhouse-Geisser	10.400	2.855	3.643	1.642	.218
	Huynh-Feldt	10.400	3.672	2.833	1.642	.202
	Lower-bound	10.400	2.000	5.200	1.642	.234
Error(ANXIETY)	Sphericity Assumed	38.000	24	1.583		
	Greenhouse-Geisser	38.000	17.127	2.219		
	Huynh-Feldt	38.000	22.030	1.725		
	Lower-bound	38.000	12.000	3.167		

Table 40

Tests of Between-Subjects Effects

Measure: ERRORS

Transformed Variable: Average

Source	Type III Sum of Squares	df	Mean Square	F	Sig.
Intercept	7605.000	1	7605.000	2258.911	.000
LEVEL	43.600	2	21.800	6.475	.012
Error	40.400	12	3.367		

Post-hoc Tukey tests are available for between-subject effects. The results show that in each condition (low, moderate, and high anxiety), advanced sport performers made significantly fewer mistakes than beginners (Table 41).

If the interaction effect in Table 39 is significant, you should proceed differently by following two steps. In step 1, carry out three separate repeated measures analyses looking at the effects of the within-subject factor (anxiety) on the number of errors in each of the competitive levels. That is, the procedure in Dialog box 34 should be repeated three times, one for each competitive level (in this case there are no between-subject factors). In order to carry out each test separately, use *Select Cases* in the *Data* menu to select the appropriate competitive level code in the data file. If any of the within-subject factor effects

Table 41

Multiple Comparisons

Measure: ERRORS
Tukey HSD

(I) LEVEL	(J) LEVEL	Mean Difference (I-J)	Std. Error	Sig.	95% Confidence Interval	
					Lower Bound	Upper Bound
beginners	intermediate	1.4000	.6700	.134	-.3875	3.1875
	advanced	2.4000*	.6700	.010	.6125	4.1875
intermediate	beginners	-1.4000	.6700	.134	-3.1875	.3875
	advanced	1.0000	.6700	.329	-.7875	2.7875
advanced	beginners	-2.4000*	.6700	.010	-4.1875	-.6125
	intermediate	-1.0000	.6700	.329	-2.7875	.7875

Based on observed means.

*. The mean difference is significant at the .05 level.

is significant, you should perform multiple paired samples *t* tests among the three anxiety conditions using the Bonferroni adjustment. For example, if you find that in the beginners group there is a significant within-subject effect, you can use *t* tests to detect which anxiety condition differs from the others.

In step 2, perform three one-way ANOVA tests (see *one-way ANOVA* in the *Analyze* menu) to examine the between-subject effects (competitive level) at the different conditions of the within-subject factor (anxiety). For example, the first ANOVA should look at whether beginners, intermediate, or advanced athletes have significant differences in the number of errors in the low anxiety condition. If any of the three ANOVA tests is significant, you should perform *post-hoc* tests or planned comparisons to examine which competitive level differs from the others in the low anxiety condition.

Figure 34 shows that the number of errors increases for all competitive levels as participants move from anxiety condition 1 (low anxiety) to anxiety condition 3 (high anxiety). As you can see, there is no significant interaction effect as the lines are parallel to each other (for an example of a significant interaction, see Figure 32).

To obtain Figure 34 you need to select *Plots* in Dialog box 78. Move *anxiety* into the *Horizontal Axis* box and *level* into the *Separate Lines* box. Click *Add* and then *Continue* (Dialog box 79).

How to report the test
When you present the results of repeated measures designs you should report the descriptive statistics in each condition. Then, for both the between and within-subjects effects as well as for the interaction effects, you should mention the *F* values, their degrees of freedom and significance levels. Where significant *F* values are found, results from *post-hoc* tests or planned comparisons should be

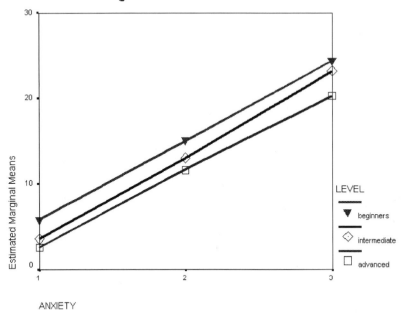

Figure 34

Dialog box 79

presented. Note that not all repeated measures designs have between-subject or interaction effects.

Example 5 shows how you could present the results of within-subject effects in repeated measures ANOVA.

Example 5: Means and standard deviations of number of errors in a complex motor skill under conditions of low, moderate, and high anxiety

Low anxiety	Moderate anxiety	High anxiety		
M(SD)	M(SD)	M(SD)	F	df
3.93_a (.20)	13.53_b (.31)	21.53_c (.55)	735.66**	2, 24

$**p < .01$

Note: Group means sharing the same subscript ($_a$, $_b$ or $_c$) in the same row are not significantly different at the $p < .05$ level.

Example 6 shows how you could present the results of between-subject effects in repeated measures ANOVA.

Example 6: Means and standard deviations of number of errors in a complex motor skill using participants with different levels of competitive experience

Beginners	Intermediate	Advanced	F	df
14.27_a (.47)	12.87_{ab} (.47)	11.87_b (.47)	6.48*	2, 12

$**p < .05$

Note: Group means sharing the same subscript ($_a$ or $_b$) in the same row are not significantly different at the $p < .05$ level.

To present interaction effects, you can create a table similar to Table 37 (including the *F* value, the degrees of freedom and the significance level of the interaction effect taken from Table 39) or, preferably, draw an interaction plot similar to Figure 34.

Correlate Bivariate

This test examines relationships between two or more variables. It is important that you are clear whether in your study you need to test for relationships or differences between variables. To examine differences, use a *t* test, a *one-way ANOVA*, a *factorial ANOVA,* or a *MANOVA* test (see the appropriate options for a description of these analyses).

Note that significant correlations do not provide sufficient evidence to argue for a causal link between variables. That is, you can say that changes in variable A relate significantly to changes in variable B, but you cannot say that variable A <u>causes</u> variable B. *Bivariate* is the simplest type of correlation. Use the

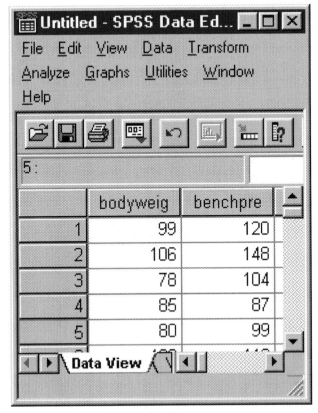

Figure 35

Pearson coefficient when you have parametric data and the *Spearman's* or *Kendall's* coefficient when you have non-parametric data (for a description of nonparametric data, see *Nonparametric Tests* in the *Analyze* menu below). Figure 35 has two columns showing body weight and maximum weight lifted in a bench press competition.

Select the two variables you want to correlate (in other examples you can select more than two variables) and move them into the *Variables* box (Dialog box 80). Then, specify whether you want a *two-tailed* or a *one-tailed* test of significance (for a distinction between the two tests, see *Independent-Samples T Test* in the *Analyze* menu). Ask SPSS to *flag significant correlations* by inserting an asterisk next to significant correlations. Use *Options* to specify how to handle missing data and to request various descriptive statistics. Click *OK* when you finish. The output is shown in Table 42

The correlation coefficient is $r = .59$, which is significant at the 0.05 level ($p = 0.036$), because it is smaller than the critical value of $p = .05$. Note that a correlation coefficient can range from -1 (perfect negative correlation) to $+1$ (perfect positive correlation). Ignore the 1.00s in the diagonal because they

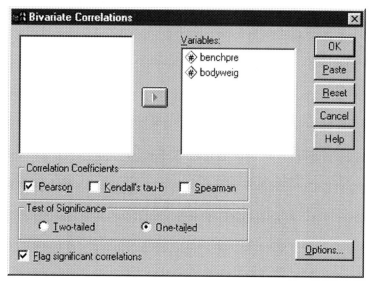

Dialog box 80

Table 42

Correlations

		BENCHPRE	BODYWEIG
BENCHPRE	Pearson Correlation	1.000	.592*
	Sig. (1-tailed)	.	.036
	N	10	10
BODYWEIG	Pearson Correlation	.592*	1.000
	Sig. (1-tailed)	.036	.
	N	10	10

*. Correlation is significant at the 0.05 level (1-tailed).

represent the correlation between a variable and itself. If you do not want SPSS to report the same correlations in both the upper and lower diagonals of the correlation matrix, use the *correlations autoscript* (see *Options* in the *Edit* menu).

When you have several variables the correlation matrix can be particularly large, because it will include the correlations between all possible combinations of the variables. However, in some cases you may be interested in some specific correlations only. For example, suppose you want to examine the relationship of performance with five different physiological and psychological indicators.

Table 43

		PERFORMA	INDI1	INDI2	INDI3	INDI4	INDI5
PERFORMA	Pearson Correlation	1.000	-.414**	.527**	-.570**	.118*	.632**
	Sig. (2-tailed)	.	.000	.000	.000	.016	.000
	N	422	415	416	422	420	422
INDI1	Pearson Correlation	-.414**	1.000	-.340**	.388**	.018	-.398**
	Sig. (2-tailed)	.000	.	.000	.000	.709	.000
	N	415	415	415	415	413	415
INDI2	Pearson Correlation	.527**	-.340**	1.000	-.468**	.054	.507**
	Sig. (2-tailed)	.000	.000	.	.000	.269	.000
	N	416	415	421	421	419	421
INDI3	Pearson Correlation	-.570**	.388**	-.468**	1.000	-.073	-.506**
	Sig. (2-tailed)	.000	.000	.000	.	.132	.000
	N	422	415	421	428	426	428
INDI4	Pearson Correlation	.118*	.018	.054	-.073	1.000	.111*
	Sig. (2-tailed)	.016	.709	.269	.132	.	.022
	N	420	413	419	426	426	426
INDI5	Pearson Correlation	.632**	-.398**	.507**	-.506**	.111*	1.000
	Sig. (2-tailed)	.000	.000	.000	.000	.022	.
	N	422	415	421	428	426	428

** Correlation is significant at the 0.01 level (2-tailed).

* Correlation is significant at the 0.05 level (2-tailed).

Suppose you are not interested in the relationships between the different indicators, but only in the relationships of these indicators with performance. To create a smaller and more manageable correlation matrix, open the Syntax window. Then type the following command:

CORRELATIONS VARIABLES = performa WITH
indi1 indi2 indi3 indi4 indi5
/MISSING = PAIRWISE
/PRINT = TWOTAIL NOSIG.

In this example it is assumed that *Performa* is your measure of performance and *indi1-5* are the five different psychological and physiological indicators. Note that you need to type a dot (.) at the end of the command line. Then go to the *Run* menu and select *All*.

Table 43 shows the full correlation matrix if you had used the *Correlate Bivariate* option. Table 44 shows that the Syntax command has created a smaller correlation matrix. Correlations between two or more variables can also be presented graphically in a scatter plot (see *Scatter* in the *Graphs* menu).

How to report the test
When you present the results of correlation analysis you should report the *r* coefficients and their significance level. Example 7 shows how you could report the results of correlation analysis in a table.

Table 44

Correlations

		INDI1	INDI2	INDI3	INDI4	INDI5
PERFORMA	Pearson Correlation	-.414**	.527**	-.570**	.118*	.632**
	Sig. (2-tailed)	.000	.000	.000	.016	.000
	N	415	416	422	420	422

**. Correlation is significant at the 0.01 level (2-tailed).

*. Correlation is significant at the 0.05 level (2-tailed).

Example 7: Correlation between body weight and maximum weight lifted in a bench-press competition

	Weight lifted
Body weight	.59*

*p < .05

Correlate Partial

Use this option to partial out the confounding effects of a third intervening variable on the relationship between two variables. In the example above, such a third intervening variable could have been the degree of previous experience in weight training. You would normally expect a positive and high correlation between body weight and weight lifted, however, the amount of lifted weight also depends on the number of years one has been practising weight training. Use partial correlations to *control for* (partial out) differences in weight training experience. Place the experience (*experien*) variable in the *Controlling for* box. Note that you can control for more than one variable. All the other options in Dialog box 81 are similar to those described in the *Bivariate Correlation* test. Click *OK*.

As you can see from Table 45, after controlling for weight training experience, the correlation between body weight and weight lifted drops from $r = .59$ (found in the *bivariate correlation* test) to $r = .49$.

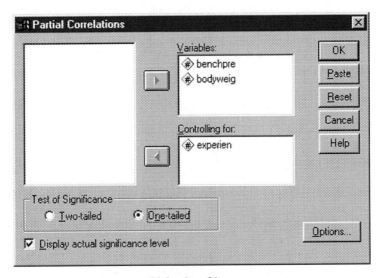

Dialog box 81

Table 45

```
- - -  P A R T I A L    C O R R E L A T I O N    C O E F F I C I E N T


Controlling for..     EXPERIEN

              BENCHPRE    BODYWEIG

BENCHPRE        1.0000        .4863
              (     0)     (      7)
               P= .         P= .092

BODYWEIG         .4863       1.0000
              (      7)     (      0)
               P= .092      P= .

(Coefficient /  (D.F.)  /  1-tailed Significance)

" . " is printed if a coefficient cannot be computed
```

How to report the test
When you present the results of partial correlation analysis you should report the *r* coefficients, their significance level, and the variable(s) whose influence is controlled.

Regression/Linear

Regression analysis is useful when you want to predict the scores of one dependent variable from the scores of one (Simple Regression) or more independent variables (Multiple Regression). Note that a significant prediction does not prove that the predictor (independent) variables have a causal effect on the predicted (dependent) variable. A significant prediction merely indicates that changes in the scores of the dependent variables can by predicted by the independent variables.

Assumptions
Tabachnick and Fidell (1996) describe a number of assumptions and important practical issues that must be taken into consideration prior to conducting a regression analysis. These are:

1. The ratio of participants to independent variables should be at least 5:1 and ideally 20:1. If the *stepwise* method is used (see below), the ratio should be 40:1. This is due to the possibility that with small sample sizes this method can produce results which do not generalise to other samples. Make sure you have enough cases (participants) in the data file, as this analysis deletes all cases with missing values. If there are not enough cases, you may need to replace the missing values with the variable mean (see *Options* below).
2. All univariate and multivariate outliers should be deleted or transformed. To detect univariate outliers, use the procedures outlined above for independent

samples *t*-test. You can also use the *Casewise diagnostics* in *Statistics* (see below). To identify outliers in the values of the dependent variable create a scatterplot of its *standardised residuals* (use *Save* below to save these residuals in the data file). To detect multivariate outliers among the independent variables, that is, cases with extreme values on a combination of variables, use the *Mahalanobis distance* or the *Leverage value* (see *Save* below).

3. The independent variables should not be very highly correlated ($r > .90$) or perfectly correlated (i.e., $r = 1$). The first condition is called multi-collinearity, the second condition is called singularity. Both conditions indicate that the independent variables contain almost identical information and, therefore, some of them should be deleted. Singularity appears when a variable is a combination (e.g., a sum or product) of other variables. To test for multicollinearity or singularity, use the *Collinearity diagnostics* in *Statistics* (see below).

4. The residuals of the regression analysis should meet the same assumptions described for ANOVA tests. See *General Linear Model/Univariate* in the *Analyze* menu for a discussion of these assumptions and how to test them. Use the *Plots* and *Save* options below to perform the residual analysis.

How to carry out the test

Suppose you have constructed a test to assess the performance of a group of athletes and you want to examine how well their performance can be predicted by measures of strength and flexibility (Figure 36).

Insert the performance measure in the *Dependent* box and the strength and flexibility measures in the *Independent(s)* box. The independent variables can be grouped into small subsets (*blocks*). To add a second subset of variables click *Next*. To move from one subset to another click *Next* and *Previous*. These subsets are required when you want to perform a hierarchical regression analysis. With this analysis, the amount of prediction of each block of independent variables is assessed separately in a sequential order (see *Change Statistics* in Table 46). The grouping of the independent variables into different blocks should be based on a certain theoretical framework or on previous research findings (Dialog box 82).

There are several methods for carrying out a regression analysis. You are advised to refer to appropriate statistical texts to find out which one suits your research design. *Enter* is a commonly used method which assesses the predictive ability of all independent variables simultaneously. Tabachnick and Fidell (1996) warn against the use of the *stepwise* method. You can specify different methods for different subsets of independent variables. Furthermore, you can limit the analysis to some cases (individuals). For example, you may want to analyse males only. Move *gender* into the *Selection Variable* box and click *Rule* (Dialog box 83). Select cases where gender=1 (assuming that this is the code you have assigned to males in the data file). Click *Continue*.

In Dialog box 82 click *Statistics* to open Dialog box 84. *Estimates of regression coefficients* offer an indication of the predictive ability of the

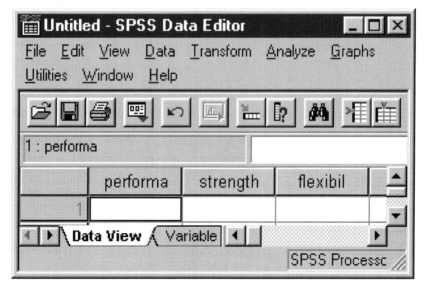

Figure 36

Dialog box 82

independent variables. *Model fit* provides a number of statistical indices
(*multiple R, R squared, adjusted R squared, F value* and its *significance* level)
which are used to evaluate the results of the regression analysis. The *R square
change* is important as it shows the change in the prediction of the dependent
variable by adding another block of independent variables. The *R square change*

Linear Regression: Set Rule

Define Selection Rule

gender   equal to   Value: 1

Continue   Cancel   Help

Dialog box 83

is particularly useful for hierarchical regression analysis. *Collinearity diagnostics* estimate whether some of the independent variables have very high correlations with other independent variables (i.e., multicollinearity). The *Durbin-Watson* test under *Residuals* tests the assumption that the residuals in the regression analysis are independent (see assumptions of residual analysis under *General Linear Model/Univariate* in the *Analyze* menu). Values that deviate from 2 indicate a non-independence of residuals. The *Durbin-Watson* test also provides a table with descriptive statistics for predicted values and residuals. Lastly, *casewise diagnostics* identifies cases with very large standardised residuals. These cases are outliers.

The *Save* option in Dialog box 82 creates new variables in the data file which can be used to examine the assumptions of regression analysis (Dialog box 85). You can save the *unstandardized* and *standardized values predicted* for each case of the dependent variable. You can also save the predicted value for a particular case when this case has not been used in the regression analysis (*adjusted*). If the predicted values change considerably you may need to revisit the particular case as it exerts a heavy influence on the results of the regression

Linear Regression: Statistics

Regression Coefficients
- ☑ Estimates
- ☐ Confidence intervals
- ☐ Covariance matrix

- ☑ Model fit
- ☑ R squared change
- ☐ Descriptives
- ☐ Part and partial correlations
- ☑ Collinearity diagnostics

Residuals
- ☑ Durbin-Watson
- ☑ Casewise diagnostics
  - ⦿ Outliers outside [3] standard deviations
  - ○ All cases

Continue   Cancel   Help

Dialog box 84

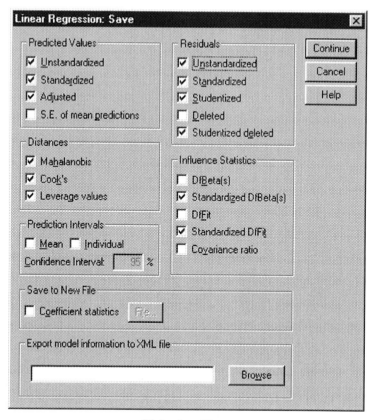

Dialog box 85

analysis. *S.E. of mean predictions* provides an estimate of the standard error of the mean predicted value. A number of different *residuals* can be saved. For a description of each residual type, see the *Save* option under *General Linear Model/Univariate* in the *Analyze* menu. *Predicted values* can be plotted against the residuals as shown for *Univariate* tests. You can also use the *Plots* option (see below) to create similar plots.

The *Save* option calculates three *distance* measures which can be used to identify influential cases among the independent variables. *Mahalanobis distance* is a measure of how much the value of a case differs in the independent variables from the average of all other cases. Large *Mahalanobis distances* signify potential outlier cases. This measure is distributed as a chi-square with degrees of freedom equal to the number of predictors. In this example, the predictors are two. Looking at the chi-square distribution table in the appendices of any statistical book, you will find that the critical value of the chi-square with 3 degrees of freedom at the $p = .01$ level is 9.21. Therefore, cases with *Mahalanobis distance* above 9.21 are potential outliers. Note that Tabachnick and Fidell (1996) suggest that this test can be used to identify outliers in other analyses (e.g., MANOVA). In such cases, the dependent variable should be a separate column in the data file with the case numbers. *Cook's distance* shows how much the regression coefficients would change if a particular case was omitted. Norusis (1998) suggests that *Cook's distances* greater than 1 usually deserve scrutiny, as they may be too influential. *Leverage values* also measure multivariate outliers. This distance measure ranges from 0 to close to 1, with greater values indicating potential outliers. Norusis (1998) suggests, as a rule of thumb, to look at values greater than $2p/N$, where p is the number of independent variables and N is the number of cases. However, this rule of thumb identifies too many cases in small samples.

The *Save* option also contains a number of *Influence Statistics*. These statistics identify cases which exert considerable influence on the calculation of various coefficients. *DfBeta(s)* show how much the regression coefficient of each independent variable and the constant term would change if a particular case was excluded from the analysis. *Standardized DfBeta(s)* contain the same information for standardised regression coefficients. Norusis (1998) proposes another rule of thumb, which states that cases should be scrutinised if they have absolute standardised values greater than $2\sqrt{N}$. *DfFit* shows the change in the predicted value of a dependent variable if a particular case is omitted. *Standardized DfFit* shows the standardised changes in the predicted values. Again, you can use the $2\sqrt{N}$ rule to identify influential cases.

In Dialog box 82 click *Plots* (Dialog box 86). This option can be used to examine the assumptions underlying the regression analysis and to identify outliers and influential cases. A number of scatterplots can be plotted using the dependent variable (*DEPENDNT*), the standardised predicted values of the dependent variable (*ZPRED*), the standardised residuals (*ZRESID*), the residuals for a case when this case is excluded from the regression (*DRESID*), the predicted value of a case when the latter is excluded from the regression (*ADJPRED*), the studentized residuals (*SRESID*), and the studentized residuals for a case when it is excluded (deleted) from the regression (*SDRESID*). To obtain a *bivariate scatterplot* with any of the above variables, move one of them into the Y box and the other into the X box. To create more than one scatterplot, use the *Next* button.

Norusis (1998) suggests a number of scatterplots to examine the assumptions of regression analysis. For example, to check the assumption of homoscedasticity, you can create a plot of *ZPRED* against the *DEPENDNT*. However, it is easier to examine this assumption if you plot the residuals against the predicted values. Norusis (1998) recommends the use of *SRESID,* as these should be normally distributed with a relatively large sample size. *SRESID* can be plotted against *ZPRED* (for an example of a similar plot, see Figure 25). Note that if you save the residuals in the data file (using the *Save* option), you could plot them against each of the independent variables. To create such plots, use the *Simple Scatterplot* in the *Graphs* menu. If the linearity assumption is met, such plots should not show any patterns. If they do, the relationship between the dependent variable and the particular independent variable is probably not linear.

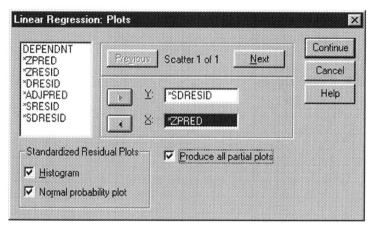

Dialog box 86

In Dialog box 86, under *Standardized Residual Plots*, you can also request a *histogram* of the standardised residuals to examine whether they are normally distributed. For example, Figure 37 shows that the residuals are relatively normally distributed.

Histogram

Dependent Variable: Performance

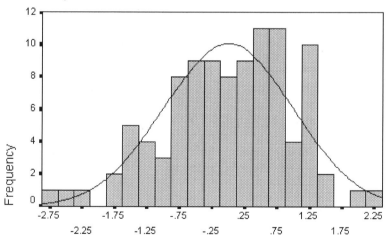

Figure 37

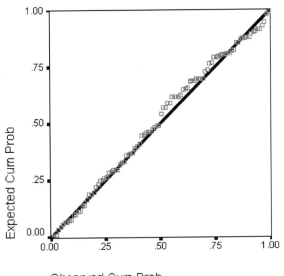

Normal P-P Plot of Regression Standardized Residual

Dependent Variable: Performance

Figure 38

The *Normal Probability Plot* shows the distribution of the standardised residuals against a standard normal distribution. As you can see from Figure 38, the distribution is more or less normal, as the points are clustered around the straight line.

Finally, in Dialog box 86 select *Produce all partial plots*. These plots can be created when there are at least two independent variables (e.g., *strength, flexibility*) in the regression. For each independent variable (e.g., *strength*), SPSS creates a scatterplot. The vertical axis of the plot shows the residuals of the dependent variable (*performance*) predicted by the other independent variable (e.g., *flexibility*). The horizontal axis of the plot shows the residuals of a regression analysis, where *strength* is now a dependent variable and *flexibility* is an independent variable. Norusis (1998) argues that by calculating the residuals in this way, you remove the linear effects of *flexibility* from both *performance* and *strength*. If the linearity assumption is met, the *partial plot* should be linear. In exactly the same way, SPSS will create another *partial plot* for *flexibility* where the vertical axis will show the residuals of *performance* predicted by *strength*, and the horizontal axis will show the residuals of *flexibility* predicted by *strength*. Figure 39 shows the first *partial plot*.

In Dialog box 82 click *Options* to open Dialog box 87. The *Stepping criteria* describe how the independent variables should be entered or removed from the analysis when a *backward, forward,* or *stepwise method* has been selected. The

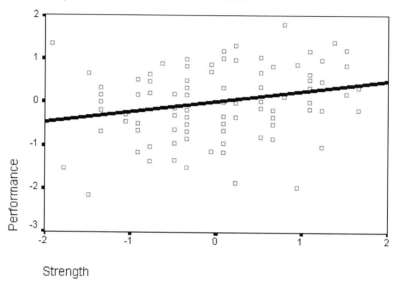

Figure 39

first criterion is based on whether the variables have reached a certain *probability* level of the *F value*. The second criterion is based on whether the variables have reached a certain *F value*. Most regression analyses should contain a *constant* term. It is therefore advisable to tick the box *include constant in the equation*. Under *Missing values* you can specify a number of different ways of handling missing values. *Exclude cases listwise* deletes all cases (participants) with missing values in any of the variables in the analysis. *Exclude cases pairwise* deletes cases with missing values only on the pair of variables used to compute the correlation coefficient on which the regression analysis is based. *Replace with mean* does not delete any cases. On the contrary, it replaces all missing values of a variable with the mean score of that variable. Use the last two options to deal with missing cases when the sample size is not large enough to provide a good ratio of cases to independent variables (see the assumptions of regression analysis above). The analysis below was carried out using both males and females.

The *R* value shows the linear association between the independent variables and the dependent variable. The *R Square* value indicates that 22% of the variance in the dependent variable is explained by the two independent variables. *Adjusted R square* represents an adjustment of the *R Square* value, as the latter is often overestimated in small sample sizes. *Change Statistics* are useful when there is more than one block of independent variables in the

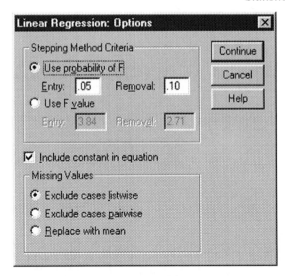

Dialog box 87

regression analysis. SPSS will show the amount of variance in the dependent variable explained by the block (*R Square Change*), and whether the variables in the new block add significantly to the prediction of the dependent variable (*F change* and its significance value).

Table 47 shows that the regression is significant ($F(2, 414) = 58.965$; $p = 0.00$), which means that the set of the two independent variables can significantly predict the dependent variable. *Residual* indicates the difference between expected and obtained scores of the dependent variable for each case. To find out whether one or both independent variables are significant predictors, you need to look at Table 48.

The standardised regression coefficient for flexibility is $b = .113$, which is significant ($t = 2.156$; $p = .032$). Similarly, the regression coefficient for strength, $b = .397$, is significant ($t = 7.564$; $p = .000$). Standardised regression coefficients range from -1 to $+1$. The higher the standardised regression coefficient (in absolute terms), the better the prediction of the dependent variable. Tolerance and VIF are produced when *Collinearity diagnostics* are selected under *Statistics* in Dialog box 84. Tolerance is the proportion of an independent variable's variance not accounted for by the other independent variables. High tolerance values indicate that there is not a problem of multicollinearity (maximum possible value is 1). In this example, the value of .681 is not very high. *VIF* (Variance Inflation Factor) represents the inverse of tolerance, and therefore high values indicate multicollinearity.

How to report the test
When you present the results of regression analysis you should first report the method of analysis used (e.g., enter). Then, report the *R* square change of each

Table 46

Model Summary[b]

Model	R	R Square	Adjusted R Square	Std. Error of the Estimate	Change Statistics					Durbin-Watson
					R Square Change	F Change	df1	df2	Sig. F Change	
1	.471[a]	.222	.218	2.0467	.222	58.965	2	414	.000	1.758

a. Predictors: (Constant), STRENGTH, FLEXIBIL

b. Dependent Variable: PERFORMA

Table 47

ANOVA[b]

Model		Sum of Squares	df	Mean Square	F	Sig.
1	Regression	493.510	2	246.755	58.965	.000[a]
	Residual	1732.481	414	4.185		
	Total	2225.990	416			

a. Predictors: (Constant), STRENGTH, FLEXIBIL

b. Dependent Variable: PERFORMA

Table 48

Coefficients[a]

Model		Unstandardized Coefficients		Standardized Coefficients	t	Sig.	Collinearity Statistics	
		B	Std. Error	Beta			Tolerance	VIF
1	(Constant)	.923	.347		2.656	.008		
	FLEXIBIL	.149	.069	.113	2.156	.032	.681	1.469
	STRENGTH	.512	.068	.397	7.564	.000	.681	1.469

a. Dependent Variable: PERFORMA

step, the *F* value of the change, its degrees of freedom and significance level. Within each step present the adjusted *R* square, the *F* value with its degrees of freedom and significance level, the standardised beta coefficients of the predictors (flexibility and strength), their *t* values and significance levels.

Example 8 shows how you could report the results of a multiple regression analysis in a table. Note that since there is only one step, the *R square change* and *F change* values are not provided.

Example 8: Prediction of performance levels from two tests of flexibility and strength

Step 1		
	b	t
Flexibility	.11*	2.16*
Strength	.40**	7.56**

*p < .05 *p < .01

Classify/Discriminant

This test is useful when you want to ascertain if some variables, measured on an interval or ratio scale, can significantly predict the categories of a nominal or interval variable.

Assumptions
According to Tabachnick and Fidell (1996), the main assumptions of this test are:

1. Normality. The predictor scores are randomly selected from the same population and are normally distributed. This assumption can be checked by using the *Descriptive Statistics/Explore* option of the *Analyze* menu. In the *Factor List* box (see Dialog box 53) insert the predicted variable, and in the *Dependent List* insert the predictor variables. With this option you can identify *outliers*, produce *normality tests*, and create *boxplots* to examine the distribution of predictor variables. To identify multivariate outliers, use the *Mahalanobis distance* measure (see below). Tabachnick and Fidell (1996) argue that discriminant analysis is relatively robust to violations of normality provided these are not caused by outliers. However, robustness requires large sample sizes.
2. Linearity. In each predicted group, all pairs of predictors should have a linear relationship. To examine this assumption, use *Matrix Scatterplots* in the *Analyze* menu. If the normality and the linearity assumptions are not met, there is an increased chance of Type II error.
3. The predictor variables should not be highly correlated with each other ($r > .90$) in order to avoid computational problems.

4. Homogeneity of variance-covariance matrices. This assumption states that variance-covariance matrices in each predicted group should be similar (i.e., come from similar populations). Results of classification analysis (see below) may well be affected by violations of this assumption. The homogeneity of variance-covariance matrices assumption can be tested by using the *Box's M* test (see below). However, this test is very sensitive and is likely to produce significant results (i.e., indicate that the homogeneity assumption cannot be accepted). You can also check this assumption by looking at the *separate group plots* (see below). Scatterplots of scores which are roughly equal in size indicate homogeneity of variance-covariance matrices. You can also request the *separate group covariance matrices* (see below) to examine whether the covariances between the predictor variables are considerably different among the predicted groups. Tabachnick and Fidell (1996) argue that discriminant analysis is relatively robust to violations of this assumption, provided that the group sizes are equal or large.

How to carry out the test
Suppose you have coded a group of gymnasts as qualifiers (code 1) and non-qualifiers (code 2) for a national competition. Also, suppose you have measured gymnasts' confidence, relaxation, and anxiety levels prior to the trials. You are interested to examine whether these three measures can distinguish between qualifiers and non-qualifiers. If they are good predictors, they will be able to maximise the differences between the two groups and classify correctly a large number of cases (gymnasts) into their appropriate groups (Figure 40).

Select the dependent variable *qualific* and move it into the *Grouping Variable* box. Click *Define Range* to define the two groups. Move the predictor variables into the *Independents* box. If you want to carry out the analysis for a subset of the sample only (e.g., females), click *Select*, identify the selection variable (i.e., gender) and type the appropriate value (e.g., 1 if this value has been used in the data file to identify females). There are two main methods of analysis: the forced entry method (*enter independents together*) and the *stepwise*. For a discussion of the advantages and disadvantages of each method, you should consult appropriate statistical texts. In Dialog box 88, the forced entry method is used.

Click on *Statistics* to open Dialog box 89. Select *Means* to produce a table with the mean scores and standard deviations of all independent variables in each group and in the whole sample. *Univariate ANOVAs* perform one-way ANOVA tests to examine whether the two groups have the same mean on each of the predictor variables. A different *ANOVA* is produced for each predictor in the discriminant model. The major discriminant predictors should have significantly different group means (i.e., the F value of the *ANOVA* should be significant). The *Box's M* is a test of the equality of the group covariance matrices (see assumptions of discriminant analysis above). The average of the covariance matrices of all groups can be requested by ticking the *within-groups covariance* matrix. Alternatively, you can ask SPSS to display the covariance matrix of each group separately (*separate-group covariance* matrix).

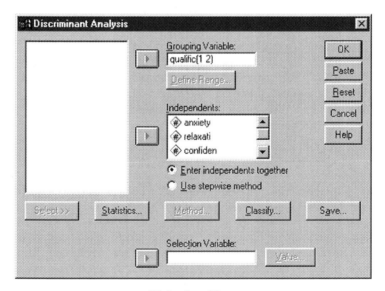

Figure 40

Dialog box 88

In Dialog box 88 click on *Classify* to open Dialog box 90. Usually, you expect that participants have equal probabilities to belong to one of the two groups, therefore you select the *All groups equal* option. However, if you want to base the calculation of probabilities on the number of cases in each group, select the *Compute from group sizes* option. *Display Casewise Results* will produce a table with the actual and predicted group membership for each case. It will also

Dialog box 89

Dialog box 90

produce the *squared mahalanobis distance to centroid* measure. Cases with large *mahalanobis distance* are potential outliers. This measure is distributed as a chi-square with degrees of freedom equal to the number of predictors. In this example, the predictors are three. Looking at the chi-square distribution table in the appendices of any statistical book, you will find that the critical value of the chi-square with three degrees of freedom at the $p = .01$ level is 11.34. Therefore, cases with *Mahalanobis distance* above 11.34 are potential outliers. *Separate groups plots* creates scatterplots for each group in order to examine the form of the relationship among pairs of predictors. If however, there is only one significant function, a histogram will be plotted instead. It is also useful to ask for a *Summary* table which will display the predictive ability of the independent variables to classify correctly the gymnasts into the two groups. Click *Continue*.

The *Save* option in Dialog box 88 adds to the data file some new variables. Specifically, for each case, it shows the group it belongs to, its discriminant score, and the probabilities of belonging to each of the two groups. Table 49 shows that two of the three *ANOVA* tests were significant, indicating that the

Table 49

Tests of Equality of Group Means

	Wilks' Lambda	F	df1	df2	Sig.
ANXIETY	.997	1.301	1	420	.255
relaxation	.978	9.477	1	420	.002
CONFIDEN	.983	7.294	1	420	.007

Table 50

Covariance Matrices

QUALIFIC		ANXIETY	relaxation	CONFIDEN
non-qualifiers	ANXIETY	.501	.349	.237
	relaxation	.349	2.117	.418
	CONFIDEN	.237	.418	.679
qualifiers	ANXIETY	.587	.447	.362
	relaxation	.447	1.977	.525
	CONFIDEN	.362	.525	.703

group means on relaxation and confidence are significantly different. Also, the *Box's M* test (not shown here) is not significant ($M = 6.41$; $F = 1.06$; $= p.384$). This indicates that the assumption of equal group covariance matrices cannot be rejected. In support of this conclusion, an inspection of the separate covariance matrices in Table 50 shows that the covariances between the pairs of variables are not very different in the two groups.

One significant function emerged which could maximise the differences between the two qualification groups in the predictors' scores. Depending on the data, multiple functions may emerge which are not always significant. In this example (Table 51) the function is significant, and therefore, you can proceed to look at the discriminant function coefficients.

Standardised canonical discriminant function coefficients (Table 52) range from −1 to +1. Coefficients above .30 (in absolute terms) are usually considered to be good predictors. In this case, relaxation and confidence are the only good predictors of the qualification status. The positive sign indicates that those who qualified had higher confidence and relaxation than those who failed to qualify. A significant discriminant function can also be interpreted by looking at the Structure Matrix (not reported here) which shows the correlations between the discriminant functions and the predictors. High correlations also indicate good predictive ability.

Table 51

Wilks' Lambda

Test of Function(s)	Wilks' Lambda	Chi-square	df	Sig.
1	.971	12.379	3	.006

Table 52

Standardized Canonical Discriminant Function Coefficients

	Function
	1
ANXIETY	-.238
relaxation	.723
CONFIDEN	.591

Table 53

Classification Results[a]

		QUALIFIC	Predicted Group Membership		Total
			non-qualifiers	qualifiers	
Original	Count	non-qualifiers	116	102	218
		qualifiers	76	128	204
		Ungrouped cases	3	1	4
	%	non-qualifiers	53.2	46.8	100.0
		qualifiers	37.3	62.7	100.0
		Ungrouped cases	75.0	25.0	100.0

a. 57.8% of original grouped cases correctly classified.

Table 53 shows that 128 (62.7%) of the qualifiers were correctly classified as being qualifiers. Also, 116 (53.2%) of the non-qualifiers were correctly classified as being non-qualifiers. Overall, 57.8% of the participants were correctly classified. The better the predictor variables the higher the percentage of correct classifications.

How to report the test
When you present the results of discriminant analysis you should first report the method of analysis used (enter or stepwise). Then present the Wilk's lambda of each discriminant function along with the chi-square value, its degrees of freedom and significance level (Table 51). Furthermore, for each significant function you should report the standardised discriminant function coefficients or the canonical correlations of the predictors (see Table 52). Finally, it is worth reporting the percentage of correct classifications.

Data Reduction/Factor

Exploratory factor analysis is an essential part of psychometric testing and validation. This analysis explores whether questionnaire items can be clustered clearly and meaningfully into small groups or factors.

Assumptions
According to Tabachnick and Fidell (1996), a number of assumptions and practical issues should be considered prior to conducting a factor analysis.

1. The sample size is large enough to provide trustworthy results. There are many contrasting opinions on what constitutes an adequate sample size. Tabachnick and Fidell (1996) propose as a rule of thumb to have at least five participants per item.
2. The data should be either interval or ratio.
3. Normality. All items and all linear combinations of items should be normally distributed. The testing of all linear combinations of items is not an easy task. However, the normality of the distribution of individual items can be assessed relatively easy (see the relevant discussion under *Compare Means/Independent-Samples T Test* above). Univariate outliers can be detected by inspecting the factor scores (see below). Factor scores outside ± 2 or ± 2.5 are possible outliers. To identify them, go to *Select cases* in the *Data* menu and in Dialog box 27 type *ABS(fac1_1)>2*. Fac1_1 is the variable which contains the factor scores of the first factor. This command will select in the data file factor scores with values above 2 or below -2. These values are potential outliers which may need to be removed. Repeat the above process for all other factors. To detect multivariate outliers, use the *Mahalanobis distance* criterion (see *Regression/Linear* in the *Analyze* menu).
4. Linearity. Relationships between pairs of items should be linear (i.e., represented by a straight line). Use the *Matrix Scatterplot* option of the *Graphs* menu to produce simple scatterplots of all possible pairs of items. If both items of a pair are normally distributed and linearly related, the scatterplot should be oval-shaped.
5. Item correlations should be of a relatively large size. If the correlations are very small (i.e., below .30), then it is questionable whether the items are

similar enough to be grouped together under some common factors. Use the *Keiser-Meyer-Olkin* test and *Bartlett's test of sphericity* (see below) to examine whether the correlations are sufficiently large to warrant a factor analysis.

If the assumptions of normality and linearity are not met, it is advisable to delete all outliers. Statisticians also suggest transformations of items to achieve normality and linearity. These transformations are beyond the scope of this book. A problem with such suggestions is that it is difficult to interpret the results of a factor analysis that contains transformed items (e.g., the logarithm of an item is not as easily interpretable as the original item).

How to carry out the test
In Figure 41, suppose you want to examine the factor structure of the Task and Ego Orientation in Sport Questionnaire (TEOSQ; see Duda 1998). The questionnaire is assumed to have two factors which represent the task and ego goal orientations.

Select the seven items that measure task orientation and the six items that measure ego orientation and move them into the *Variables* box (Dialog box 91). If you want to carry out the analysis with part of the sample only, you can specify certain selection criteria. For example, you can specify that the *Selection Variable* will be gender and that you will only use *Values* where *gender = 1*, that is only males (assuming that you have assigned this code to males in the data file).

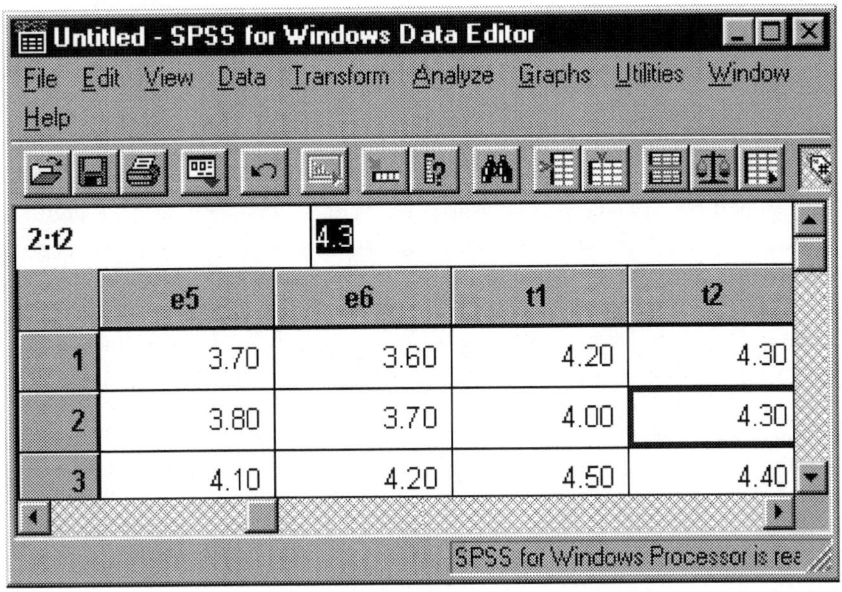

Figure 41

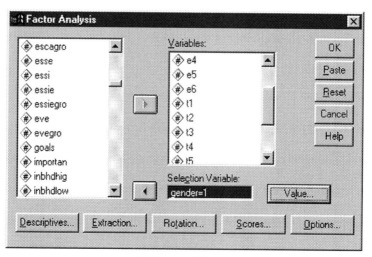

Dialog box 91

In the *Descriptives* make sure that you tick the *Initial Solution* box to obtain the initial statistics before the solution is rotated (Dialog box 92). The *KMO* (Keiser-Meyer-Olkin) and *Bartlett's test of sphericity* can be used to examine assumptions relating to the appropriateness of the factor analysis. The *KMO* is a measure of sampling adequacy and examines the degree of correlation among the questionnaire items. Values above .60 are considered acceptable. *Bartlett's test of sphericity* is another measure of the appropriateness of factor analysis. It tests whether the correlations among the items are sufficiently high to indicate the existence of factors. However, this test is not very informative as it is often found to be significant (i.e., indicating the existence of factors) in large sample sizes, even if the actual correlations are low.

Use *Extraction* in Dialog box 91 to indicate the method of factor analysis. Three methods are usually employed in the literature (see Dialog box 93): *Principal components, Principal axis factoring*, and *Maximum Likelihood*. For a discussion of the advantages and disadvantages of each method, you are advised to refer to appropriate statistical texts. In *Display, tick the Unrotated factor solution* to display the unrotated factor loadings (i.e., correlations between items and a factor) and an indicator of the variance explained by the factors (*Eigenvalues*). The *Scree plot* is useful for deciding how many factors should represent the items. The plot is derived by plotting the *eigenvalues* against the number of factors extracted (see Figure 42). After the first factor, the plot starts to slope steeply downwards, but then straightens out. The point in the *x*-axis before the line straightens out is taken to indicate the appropriate number of factors.

Besides the scree plot, there are two other means by which you can determine the number of factors in a factor analysis. The first selects only those factors with *Eigenvalues* greater than 1(free solution). Alternatively, you can specify the

Dialog box 92

number of factors to be extracted. In the present example, you could specify two factors, because a task and an ego goal orientation factor are expected. The latter option is often called a forced solution, because you impose on the data the desired number of factors. A forced solution usually explains less item variance than a free solution. Dialog box 93 lists at the bottom the *maximum iterations for* factor extraction. By default these are 25, which should be enough to provide a good solution (i.e., to achieve *convergence*). You can increase the number of iterations if the solution cannot converge, although a relatively large number of iterations can raise questions regarding the appropriateness of the solution. Click *Continue*.

With *Rotation* (see Dialog box 91) the factors are fine-tuned in order to achieve a simple and meaningful solution. Two of the most commonly employed methods of rotation are: *Varimax*, used when the factors are hypothesised to be unrelated, and *Direct Oblimin*, used when the factors are hypothesised to be correlated. In Dialog box 94, the task and ego goal orientation factors are hypothesised by the achievement goal theory to be unrelated, therefore a *Varimax* solution is selected. Tick the *Display rotated solution* option to produce the final factor loadings after the rotation. Finally, click *Continue*.

Scores in Dialog box 91 allows you to save new variables in the data file which contain the estimates of the scores participants would have allocated to each factor if it had been measured directly. These *factor scores* are standardized (use the *regression* method). A separate variable is created in the data file for each factor of the rotated solution. *Options* in Dialog box 91 specify the way *missing values* should be handled (see Dialog box 95). For an easier interpretation of a factor solution (especially if you are analysing a large number of items), it is useful to ask SPSS to *sort by size* the factor loadings. Also, because most statistical texts suggest that factor loadings below .30 indicate poor factorial structure, it is recommended that such loadings are

Dialog box 93

Dialog box 94

suppressed (hidden) in the output. Click *Continue*, and when you get back to Dialog box 91, click *OK*.

The output presents first the *KMO* measure of sampling adequacy and *Bartlett's test of sphericity*. The results (not presented here) indicate that the *KMO* is satisfactorily high (.78), and that the *Bartlett's test* is significant ($x^2(78) = 1505.38; < .05$). Taken together, the tests show that factor analysis is appropriate with these items as their intercorrelations are substantially large.

Table 54 presents the unrotated solution. Thirteen factors were extracted which cumulatively explained 100% of the variance. However, only the first two factors were retained because they had eigenvalues greater than 1 (remember that a free solution was specified). The *Rotation Sums of Squared Loadings* show the eigenvalues (*total*) and the *percentage of variance* explained by the two factors after their rotation. Factors 1 and 2 explained 21.6% and 20.6% of the item variance respectively. *Cumulatively*, the two factors explained 42.2% of

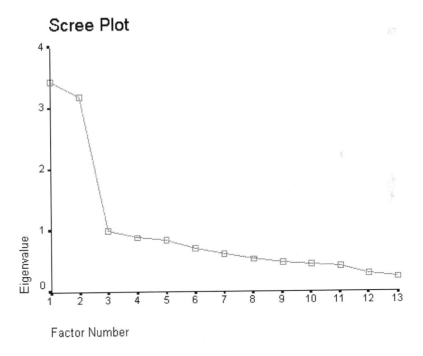

Dialog box 95

Scree Plot

Figure 42

the variance. The Scree Plot (Figure 42) also supports the conclusion that there are only two factors, because the plotted line straightens out after the first two factors.

The rotated factor matrix in Table 55 shows that the two-factor solution has high factor loadings. All the ego goal orientation items have been grouped together to form an ego orientation factor, and similarly, all the task goal

Table 54

Total Variance Explained

Factor	Initial Eigenvalues			Extraction Sums of Squared Loadings			Rotation Sums of Squared Loadings		
	Total	% of Variance	Cumulative %	Total	% of Variance	Cumulative %	Total	% of Variance	Cumulative %
1	3.422	26.321	26.321	2.881	22.158	22.158	2.818	21.677	21.677
2	3.173	24.409	50.730	2.617	20.129	42.287	2.679	20.611	42.287
3	.997	7.670	58.400						
4	.880	6.768	65.168						
5	.838	6.448	71.616						
6	.699	5.374	76.990						
7	.617	4.750	81.739						
8	.528	4.059	85.798						
9	.478	3.674	89.472						
10	.435	3.346	92.818						
11	.405	3.113	95.931						
12	.293	2.253	98.184						
13	.236	1.816	100.000						

Extraction Method: Principal Axis Factoring.

Table 55

Rotated Factor Matrix[a]

	Factor	
	1	2
E3	.808	
E2	.795	
E6	.642	
E4	.638	
E1	.626	
E5	.542	
T5		.717
T3		.688
T4		.628
T1		.620
T7		.581
T6		.578
T2		.450

Extraction Method: Principal Axis Factoring.
Rotation Method: Varimax with Kaiser Normalization.
a. Rotation converged in 3 iterations.

orientation items have been grouped together to form a task orientation factor. This is a clear factor structure with no crossloadings (i.e., items loading on more than one factor).

Note that when an oblique method of rotation is used, factor loadings appear both in a pattern matrix and in a structure matrix. Statisticians (e.g., Kline, 1994) recommend that you should examine the structure matrix because its loadings represent the item-factor correlations and it can be interpreted more easily.

How to report the test
When you present a factor analysis you should first report the results from the *KMO* measure of sampling adequacy. Then describe the methods used for factor

rotation and factor extraction. For each extracted factor, present its eigenvalue and the percentage of variance it explains. It is also worth reporting the total percentage of variance explained by all extracted factors. Finally, present the scree test and the item loadings in the rotated factor matrix or structure matrix (see Table 55).

Scale/Reliability Analysis

Reliability analysis measures the internal consistency of a group of items. This analysis is frequently used in questionnaire construction. Often, questionnaires have more than one scale. Reliability analysis examines the homogeneity or cohesion of the items that comprise each scale. Cronbach's alpha coefficient (α) is the most frequently used index of reliability, although other indices are also used (e.g., *split-half* reliability). Alpha coefficients reflect the average correlation among the items that constitute a scale. Ideally, alphas should be between .70 and .90. Low alphas indicate poor internal consistency of a scale, because the items that make up the scale are poorly related to each other. Very high alphas indicate that the items are almost identical (and perhaps redundant) and, therefore, the generic meaning of the scale is too narrow. Note that the number of items in a scale can affect the size of the alpha coefficient. For example, a scale may have an alpha of .60 because it consists of only three items. If this is the case, by increasing the number of items to four or five, the alpha coefficient can rise to .70 or above, provided that none of the items correlates poorly with the rest (see *alpha if item deleted* in Table 56). Sometimes, the alpha coefficient is negative indicating that the items are very poorly correlated. However, often the reason for the negative alpha is the inclusion of an item which has not been recoded (see *Recode into different variables* in the *Transform* menu). Figure 43 tests whether a proposed enjoyment scale, consisting of five enjoyment items, has adequate internal consistency.

Select Cronbach's *alpha* coefficient from the available list (*Model*). Make sure that you tick the *Descriptives for scale if item deleted* option in the *Statistics* dialog box (see Dialog box 97) because, as you will see below, it is a very useful option. When you finish, go back to Dialog box 96 and click *OK*. Table 56 shows part of the output.

As can be seen, the alpha coefficient is acceptable ($\alpha = .86$). It is always useful to look at the *corrected item-total correlations*. Low corrected correlations indicate that the particular item is problematic and perhaps it should be removed. It is called *corrected item-total correlation* because the total is composed of all scale items except the one it is correlated with. Problematic items can also be detected by looking at the new alpha of the scale if an *item is deleted*. If the alpha increases considerably with the deletion of a particular item, it might be appropriate to delete that item.

The *Reliability Analysis* option provides another useful coefficient, the *intraclass correlation coefficient*. This coefficient compares changes in the mean scores of a variable over multiple measures. In other words, it estimates

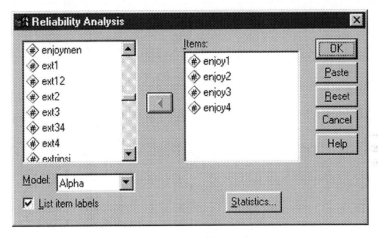

Figure 43

Dialog box 96

the reliability of a measure over time. Statisticians (e.g., Vincent, 1999) argue that the *intraclass correlation coefficient* is a more appropriate indicator of test-retest reliability compared to the *Pearson's* correlation coefficient (see *Correlate Bivariate* in the *Analyze* menu).

In Figure 44, suppose you want to examine whether five judges in gymnastics are consistent in their rating of five different gymnasts. The interest is on the consistency of the judges' scores (i.e., good performances receive higher scores than average or poor performances) rather than their absolute agreement (i.e., identical scores for the same gymnast). In other words, you are looking for non-significant differences across the columns of Figure 44. Move the variables *judge1-5* in the *Items* box of Dialog box 96. Then click *Statistics*.

Table 56

```
Item-total Statistics
                Scale          Scale       Corrected
                Mean         Variance        Item-            Alpha
              if Item        if Item         Total          if Item
              Deleted        Deleted      Correlation        Deleted
ENJOY1        15.0123        21.1994         .6866            .8256
ENJOY2        15.2408        20.7054         .7182            .8129
ENJOY3        14.8452        20.1361         .6498            .8427
ENJOY4        14.7027        19.1602         .7611            .7933

Reliability Coefficients
N of Cases =      407.0                    N of Items =    4
Alpha =       .8578
```

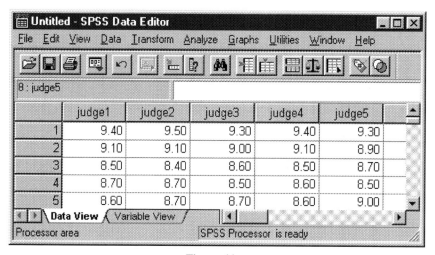

Figure 44

Select the *intraclass correlation coefficient*. Choose the *two-way random model*, as there are two sources of variation in the study (i.e., variation of scores due to different gymnasts, and variation of scores due to different judges). A *two-way random model* is used because it is assumed that the judges are a random sample of a larger population of judges. If the sample is not random, select a *mixed* model. You should select a *one-way random* model if you do not know which scores were given by which judge. The *ANOVA table* tests whether there are any significant differences among the mean scores of the five judges (i.e., whether the judges are consistent). Use the *F* test if you have parametric data (such as the one in this example), and the *Friedman chi-square* if you have non-parametric data. Click *Continue*, and when you go back to Dialog box 96, click *OK*.

Table 57 shows that the judges are very consistent, as the *F* value in the *Analysis of Variance* is not significant, and the *average measure intraclass correlation* is .975. Values above .70 are considered acceptable (Vincent, 1999). Note, that the significant *F* value ($F (4, 16) = 39.96$; $p = .000$) under the *average*

Dialog box 97

measure intraclass correlation is not surprising, because it indicates that there are significant differences in the scores of different gymnasts (i.e., differences across the rows of Figure 44). The *single measure intraclass correlation* shows the reliability if only one judge was used. Usually, this reliability is lower than the reliability obtained from multiple judges (i.e., *average measure intraclass correlation*).

Table 57

```
Analysis of Variance

Source of Variation    Sum of Sq.     DF    Mean Square   F      Prob.

Between People          2.4616         4      .6154
Within People            .2600        20      .0130
  Between Measures       .0136         4      .0034      .2208  .9229
  Residual               .2464        16      .0154
Total                   2.7216        24      .1134
       Grand Mean       8.8560

              Intraclass Correlation Coefficient

Two-Way Random Effect Model (Consistency Definition):
People and Measure Effect Random
  Single Measure Intraclass Correlation =    .8863*
     95.00% C.I.:           Lower =   .6602      Upper =    .9857
  F = 39.9610   DF = (    4,   16.0)   Sig. = .0000   (Test Value = .0000)
  Average Measure Intraclass Correlation =    .9750
     95.00% C.I.:           Lower =   .9067      Upper =    .9971
  F = 39.9610   DF = (    4,   16.0)   Sig. = .0000   (Test Value = .0000)
*: Notice that the same estimator is used whether the interaction effect
   is present or not.
```

Nonparametric Tests/Chi-square

This test is employed to compare two or more categories of one or more variables. For example, you may want to examine whether a sample of 100 pupils differ in their choice of favourite football club. After carrying out a frequency count, you find out that 32 pupils support club A, 26 support club B, 19 support club C, 14 support club D, and 9 support club E. In the data file you can create a variable with 100 cases (rows) that will represent the club preference of each pupil. Alternatively, you can create another variable (*clubs*) with five rows. Type in the total number of preferences for each of the five clubs, and then use the *weight cases* option of the *Data* menu to indicate that each row represents a total score rather than an individual case (Figure 45).

Move the *clubs* variable into the *Test variable list* (Dialog box 98). Use *Options* to ask for descriptive statistics and specify how to handle missing values. If you want to restrict the comparison to, say, the first three clubs only (A, B, and C), select *use specified range* under *Expected Range* and type 1 and 3 as the *Lower* and *Upper* values. Then click *OK*.

The output in Table 58 shows the observed number of preferences for each club. If there were no significant differences in club preference, the expected number of preferences for each club would have been 20. The chi-square test examines the significance of the differences between the expected and the actual (observed) preferences.

The results show that the chi-square value ($x^2(4) = 16.9$) is significant ($p = .002$), which means that there is a significant difference in club preference (Table 59). Club A is the most popular club and club E is the least popular. *Residual* represent the difference between the observed and expected frequencies. For a chi-square analysis, a relatively large sample size is

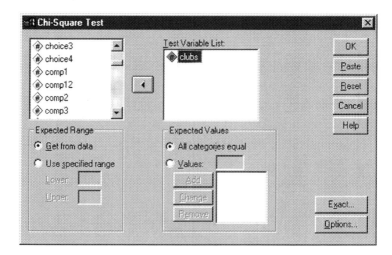

Dialog box 98

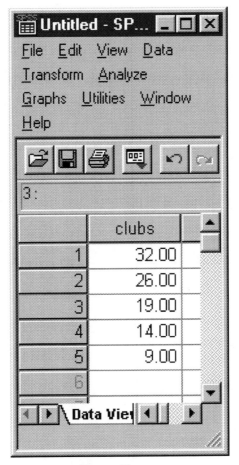

Figure 45

necessary. Results may be inappropriate if there are less than five expected frequencies in any of the categories (i.e., football clubs).

In some cases you may not want to assign equal expected frequencies to all categories. In the example of Table 59, suppose you have obtained results from a much larger survey and you want to examine whether there are any significant differences in club preference between this study and the larger survey. Under *Expected Values* use *Add* to specify the frequencies for each club as they were reported in the larger survey. The new values are *33* for Club A, *25* for club B, *21* for Club C, *16* for club D, and *5* for Club E. The order in which you enter the new values is crucial. Firstly, identify the smallest value (i.e. 9) of the test variable *clubs*. In the *Values* box enter its corresponding new value (i.e 5). Click *Add* and the new value will appear at the bottom of the value list. Repeat the same process with the remaining variables. The sequential order of the new values is important; it must correspond to the ascending order of the values of

Table 58

CLUBS

	Observed N	Expected N	Residual
Club A	32	20.0	12.0
Club B	26	20.0	6.0
Club C	19	20.0	-1.0
Club D	14	20.0	-6.0
Club E	9	20.0	-11.0
Total	100		

Table 59

Test Statistics

	CLUBS
Chi-Square^a	16.900
df	4
Asymp. Sig.	.002

a. 0 cells (.0%) have expected frequencies less than 5.
The minimum expected cell frequency is 20.0.

the test variable *clubs*. That is, enter the new value for Club E first, and then for Club D, Club C, Club B, and finally for Club A. Then click *OK* (Dialog box 99).

As Table 60 shows, the chi-square value is non-significant (x^2 (4) = 3.71; $p = .447$) and, therefore, you should conclude that there are no significant differences in club preference between this study and the larger survey.

Table 61 shows the difference in preferences for each club recorded in this study (Observed Frequencies) and the larger survey (Expected Frequencies)

If you want to examine differences among the categories of more than one variable, you cannot use this option. An alternative way to calculate the chi-square statistic can be found in the *Summarize Crosstabs* option of the *Analyze* menu. Suppose you want to examine whether the observed differences in the first example are due to the different gender of the pupils. Figure 46 has two

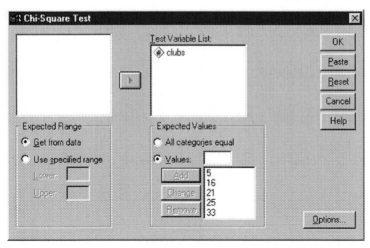

Dialog box 99

Table 60

Test Statistics

	CLUBS
Chi-Square[a]	3.711
df	4
Asymp. Sig.	.447

a. 0 cells (.0%) have expected frequencies less than 5. The minimum expected cell frequency is 5.0.

Table 61

CLUBS

	Observed N	Expected N	Residual
Club E	9	5.0	4.0
Club D	14	16.0	-2.0
Club C	19	21.0	-2.0
Club B	26	25.0	1.0
Club A	32	33.0	-1.0
Total	100		

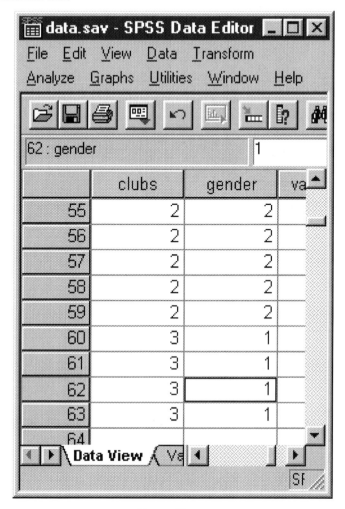

Figure 46

columns: *clubs* which presents the club preferences of each participant, and *gender* (1 = females, 2 = males).

In the *crosstabs* dialog box move one of the variables in the *Row(s)* box and the other in the *Column(s)* box. Click *Statistics* and select *chi-square*. Click *Continue*, and then *OK* (Dialog box 100).

Tables 62 and 63 below present the crosstabulation of male and female club preferences. The chi-square value is not significant ($x^2(4) = .446$; $p = .979$). Therefore, you should conclude that there are no gender differences in club preferences.

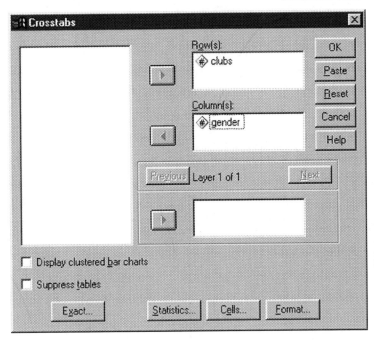

Dialog box 100

Table 62

CLUBS * GENDER Crosstabulation

Count

		GENDER		
		females	males	Total
CLUBS	Club A	14	18	32
	Club B	12	14	26
	Club C	9	10	19
	Club D	7	7	14
	Club E	6	5	11
Total		48	54	102

Table 63

Chi-Square Tests

	Value	df	Asymp. Sig. (2-sided)
Pearson Chi-Square	.446[a]	4	.979
Likelihood Ratio	.446	4	.979
Linear-by-Linear Association	.422	1	.516
N of Valid Cases	102		

a. 0 cells (.0%) have expected count less than 5. The minimum expected count is 5.18.

How to report the test
When you present the results of a chi-square analysis you should report the observed and expected frequencies for each category, the chi-square value, its *df* and significance level. Example 9 shows how you could report the results of a chi-square test in a table.

Example 9: Differences in the choice of favourite football club among a sample of pupils

	Observed *N*	Expected *N*	x^2	*df*
Club A	32	20	16.9*	4
Club B	26	20		
Club C	19	20		
Club D	14	20		
Club E	9	20		

*$p < .05$

Nonparametric Tests/2 Independent Samples
This test is the non-parametric equivalent to the *Independent-Samples T Test*. Nonparametric tests are appropriate when using ordinal scales (i.e., ranks rather than raw data), or when the data are measured on an interval or ratio scale but do not meet the assumptions of parametric tests. Suppose you conduct an experiment to examine whether a new brand of trainers can help to improve the performance of twelve runners. The performance measure is their ranking in a 100m race. Suppose you assign the code 1 to the first six runners who run with

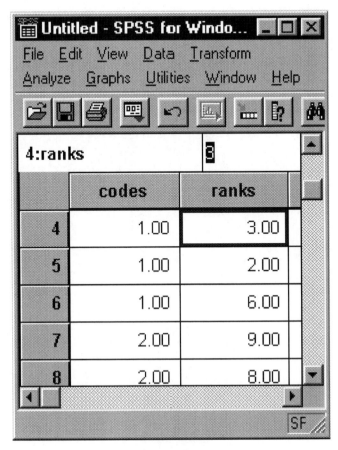

Figure 47

the new brand of trainers, and the code 2 to the other six runners who run with conventional trainers (Figure 47).

The dependent variable is the ranking of the runners (*ranks*) and it should be moved into the *Test Variable List* box. The independent variable (*codes*) has the codes for the two groups and it should be moved in the *Grouping Variable* box (Dialog box 101).

Click on *Define Groups* to specify the two groups shown in Dialog box 102.

The *Mann-Whitney U* test is the most commonly employed test for *2 independent samples*. Use *Options* to indicate the way you would like to handle missing data and to ask for some descriptive statistics. Finally, click *OK*.

As you can see in Table 64, the mean rank of the first group is lower than the mean rank of the second group. This indicates that those who wore the new pair of trainers ran faster. However, you need to find out whether the difference in the mean ranks between the two groups is significant.

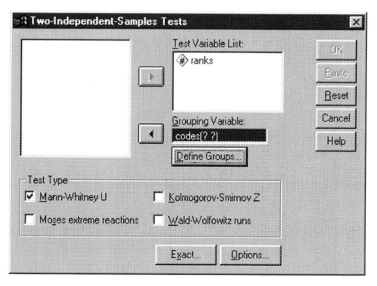

Dialog box 101

Dialog box 102

Table 65 shows that the *U* value of 3 is significant ($p = 0.015$). Note that the significance level for one-tailed *t* test is chosen, because it is expected that the two groups will differ in a particular direction (that is, those with the new trainers are expected to run faster; see Vincent, 1999). Because the *U* value is significant, you can conclude that the mean rank of those runners who wore the new trainers was significantly lower than the mean rank of those who wore the old trainers.

How to report the test

When you present the results of a Mann-Whitney *U* test you should report the mean rank of each group, the *U* value and its significance level.

Example 10 shows how you could report the results of a Mann-Whitney *U* test in a table.

Table 64

Ranks

CODES	N	Mean Rank	Sum of Ranks
RANKS 1.00	6	4.00	24.00
2.00	6	9.00	54.00
Total	12		

Table 65

Test Statistics[b]

	RANKS
Mann-Whitney U	3.000
Wilcoxon W	24.000
Z	-2.402
Asymp. Sig. (2-tailed)	.016
Exact Sig. [2*(1-tailed Sig.)]	.015[a]

a. Not corrected for ties.

b. Grouping Variable: CODES

Example 10: Mean ranking in a 100 m race of runners with new and conventional trainers

	M rank	U
Group 1 (New trainers)	4	3*
Group 2 (Conventional trainers)	9	

*p < .05

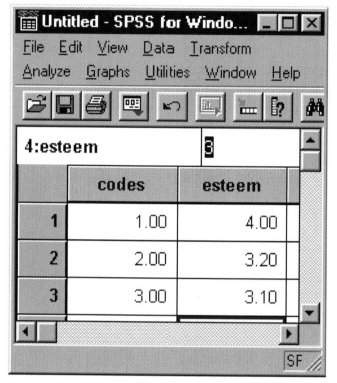

Figure 48

Nonparametric Tests/K Independent Samples

This is an extension of the previous test. It is used when the independent variable has more than two groups. In Figure 48, it is assumed that you have measured the body self-esteem (e.g., on a 5-point Likert scale) of participants who practise weight training (code 1), aerobics (code 2), and tennis (code 3). The sample consists of 15 participants.

The most appropriate analysis for this design is *one-way ANOVA*. However, suppose that the assumptions of that test are not met. In this case, it is best to use the *K independent samples* test, which is the non-parametric equivalent of *one-way ANOVA*. SPSS will automatically convert the raw self-esteem scores into ranks. Select the dependent variable *esteem* and move it into the *Test Variable List* (you can carry out more than one test by moving into this box a number of different dependent variables). Move the independent variable *codes* into the *Grouping Variable* box and click on *Define Range* to define groups 1–3. Usually, researchers use the *Kruskal-Wallis H* test to carry out the *K independent samples* test. Use *Options* to ask for descriptive statistics and to specify how to handle missing values. Finally, click *OK* (Dialog box 103).

As the results show (Table 66), those who do weight training have a higher mean rank (i.e., higher body self-esteem) than the other two groups. The chi-

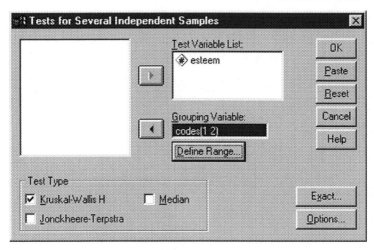

Dialog box 103

square value of the *Kruskal-Wallis* test is x^2 (2) = 7.85, which is significant ($p = 0.020$) (Table 67). Therefore, you should conclude that the mean ranks of the three groups in body self-esteem differ significantly from each other.

Unfortunately, SPSS does not offer *post-hoc* tests, similar to those offered in *one-way ANOVA*. To locate where the significant differences lie, use the formulae on page 205 in Thomas and Nelson's (1996) book. Alternatively, you can carry out three *Mann-Whitney U* tests (see *Nonparametric tests-2 independent samples* in the *Analyze* menu) comparing group 1 with group 2, group 2 with group 3, and group 1 with group 3. For these multiple comparisons the significance level should be adjusted by dividing the conventional .05 level with the number of tests (i.e., 3). Therefore, the new significance level for the multiple comparisons should be $p = 017$. The three *Mann-Whitney U* tests show

Table 66

Ranks

	CODES	N	Mean Rank
ESTEEM	weight training	5	11.90
	aerobics	5	7.90
	tennis	5	4.20
	Total	15	

Table 67

Test Statistics[a],[b]

	ESTEEM
Chi-Square	7.850
df	2
Asymp. Sig.	.020

a. Kruskal Wallis Test

b. Grouping Variable: CODES

that the only significant difference was between those who practise weightlifting (group 1) and tennis (group 3), with the former having significantly higher mean rank (i.e., higher body self-esteem). Groups 1 and 2, and groups 2 and 3 do not differ significantly from each other.

How to report the test
When you present the results of a *Kruskal-Wallis* test you should report the mean rank of each group, the chi-square value, its degrees of freedom and significance level.

Example 11 shows how you could report the results of a *Kruskal-Wallis* test in a table.

Example 11: Differences in self-esteem among participants from three types of sport

	M rank	x^2	df
Weight training	11.90	7.85*	2
Aerobics	7.90		
Tennis	4.20		

$*p < .05$

Nonparametric Tests/2 Related Samples

This test is the nonparametric equivalent of *Paired Samples T Test*. It is used when the same group of people is tested twice. Suppose you want to examine whether mental practice can reduce the number of errors in a complex motor skill (Figure 49).

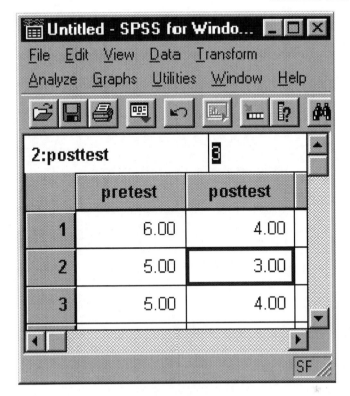

Figure 49

Owing to the fact that the data do not meet the assumptions of the parametric *t* test, you decide to use the equivalent nonparametric *2 Related Samples* test. SPSS will convert automatically the raw data into ranks. Select the *pretest* and *posttest* variables and move them into the *Test pair(s) list* box. *The Wilcoxon* test is the most commonly employed test for *2 related samples*. Use *Options* to ask for descriptive statistics and specify how to handle missing values. Finally, click *OK* (Dialog box 104).

As can be seen in Table 68, there are seven negative ranks. In this example, the negative ranks indicate that the participants made more errors in the first condition, that is, before using mental practice. The positive rank indicates that one participant made more errors after using mental practice. Finally, for two participants the number of errors did not change across the two conditions (i.e., there were 2 ties).

The *Wilcoxon* test has a value of $z = -2.126$, which is significant (significance or $p = .033$ (Table 69)). Therefore, you should conclude that mental practice reduced the number of errors in the complex motor skill, because the mean ranks of the two conditions differed significantly from each other.

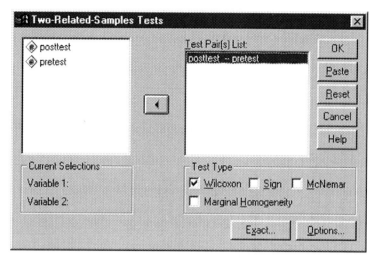

Dialog box 104

Table 68

Ranks

		N	Mean Rank	Sum of Ranks
POSTTEST - PRETEST	Negative Ranks	7ᵃ	4.64	32.50
	Positive Ranks	1ᵇ	3.50	3.50
	Ties	2ᶜ		
	Total	10		

a. POSTTEST < PRETEST

b. POSTTEST > PRETEST

c. PRETEST = POSTTEST

How to report the test

When you present the results of a *Wilcoxon* test you should report the mean rank of each condition (before and after mental practice), the z value and its significance level.

Example 12 shows how you could report the results of a *Wilcoxon* test in a table.

Example 12: Number of errors in a complex motor skill before and after mental practice

	M rank	z
Before mental practice	4.64	2.12*
After mental practice	3.50	

*$p < .05$

Table 69

Test Statistics[b]

	POSTTEST-PRETEST
Z	-2.126[a]
Asymp. Sig. (2-tailed)	.033

a. Based on positive ranks.

b. Wilcoxon Signed Ranks Test

Nonparametic Tests/K Related Samples

This test is an extension of the *2 Related Samples* test and it is used when the same group of individuals is assessed more than twice. This test is the nonparametric equivalent of *Repeated Measures ANOVA*. Suppose you have asked eight participants to rank three different sport celebrities in order of prestige. The participants have to give a different rank to each celebrity. The three celebrities represent the three repeated conditions (Figure 50).

Move the three celebrities (*a*, *b*, and *c*) into the *Test Variables* box (Dialog box 105). Select *Statistics* if you want to calculate the mean, standard deviation, minimum, maximum, and the number of complete cases. Select the *Friedman* test and click *OK*.

Table 70 shows the mean ranks for each sport celebrity. To find out whether these means differ significantly from each other, you need to look at the chi-square value. In Table 71 the chi-square is non-significant (x^2 (2) = .25; $p = .882$). Therefore, you should conclude that the participants in this study do not rank differently the three sport celebrities.

How to report the test
When you present the results of a *Friedman* test you should report the mean rank of each condition (celebrities *a*, *b*, and *c*), the chi-square value, its degrees of freedom and significance level. Example 13 shows how you could present the results of a *Friedman* test.

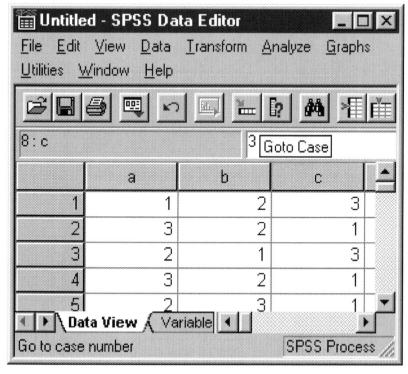

Figure 50

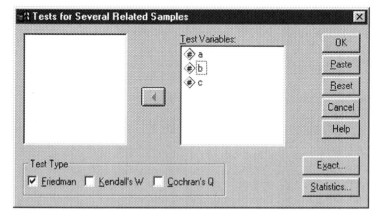

Dialog box 105

Table 70

Ranks

	Mean Rank
A	2.13
B	2.00
C	1.88

Table 71

Test Statistics[a]

N	8
Chi-Square	.250
df	2
Asymp. Sig.	.882

a. Friedman Test

Example 13: Differences in the ranking of three sport celebrities in order of prestige

	M rank	x^2	*df*
Celebrity A	2.13	.25 (n.s.)	2
Celebrity B	2.00		
Celebrity C	1.88		

4 Chart and table options

Graphs

SPSS offers a wide variety of charts which can be useful in exploring and summarising your data. Some of these graphs will be presented here.

Bar

This is one of the most commonly used types of chart. Bars can represent different categories of a variable or different variables. SPSS offers three types of bar chart: *Simple, clustered*, and *stacked* (Dialog box 106). For each type, charts can be produced for *groups of cases, separate variables*, or *individual cases.*

Summaries for groups of cases
This option summarises the different categories of a variable, sometimes within a *summary function* (e.g., mean score) of a second variable. Click *Simple* and *Define*.

Suppose you want to plot a chart showing the different sports practised by a group of pupils (Dialog box 107).

The sports are listed within a variable called *activity*. Move this variable into the *Category Axis* box. Click *Title*. In Dialog box 108, you can give a *title*, a *subtitle*, or a *footnote* to the bar chart. Click *Continue*.

Options in Dialog box 107 lets you specify whether you want any missing values to appear as a separate category (bar) in the chart. Figure 51 presents a frequency count (*N of cases*) of each sport. The most popular sport in this sample is football.

In Dialog box 107, bars can represent the *number of cases* (as above), *cumulative number of cases*, or *percentages* for the different categories (i.e., sports) of the *activity* variable. In addition, you can summarise the different categories of *activity* within a function of a second variable. For example, you can show that pupils who play different sports have different enjoyment scores. From dialog box 109, select *Other summary function* under the *Bars Represent* option. Move the *enjoy* variable in the *Variable* box. SPSS will calculate the mean score of this variable unless you change the *summary function* (see below). Click *OK*.

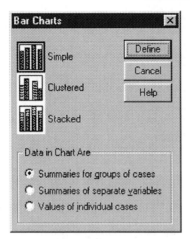

Dialog box 106

Dialog box 107

As Figure 52 shows, on the average pupils enjoyed mostly rounders and badminton.

You can request other summary functions besides the mean. In Dialog box 109, click *Change Summary*. A number of functions are available. For example, if the enjoyment scale ranges from 1 ('I don't enjoy this sport at all') to 7 ('I enjoy this sport very much'), you can select the *Number above* option (e.g., 5), and SPSS will show how many pupils from each sport scored 5 or above in the enjoyment scale (Dialog box 110).

For example, Figure 53 demonstrates that 48 pupils who played football scored 5 or above in the enjoyment scale.

Dialog box 108

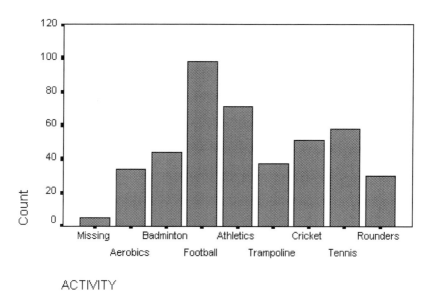

Figure 51

You can also find out how many pupils fell within a certain range of enjoyment scores. At the bottom of Dialog box 110 select *Number inside* and type *Low* 1 and *High* 2. For example, Figure 54 below shows that 14 pupils who did athletics scored between 1 and 2 in the enjoyment scale.

With *clustered* charts you can categorise levels of one variable within the categories of a second variable (rather than within a *function* of the second variable as in *simple bar* charts). Suppose you want to find out what percentages of males and females play each of the above types of sport. Click *clustered* in

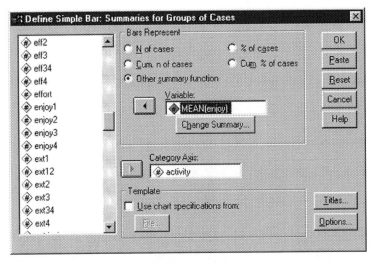

Dialog box 109

Dialog box 110

Dialog box 106. Move *activity* into the *Category axis* box and *gender* into the *Define clusters by* box. All other options are similar to the ones described for *simple bar* charts. Click *OK* (Dialog box 111).

For example, Figure 55 shows that 23 males and 12 females practised trampoline.

Sports practised by study participants

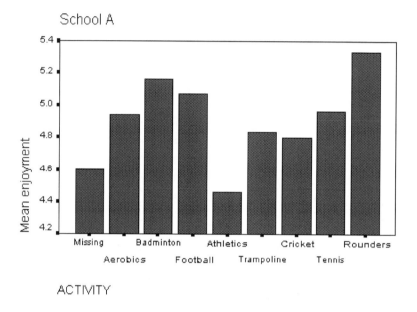

Figure 52

Figure 52 plotted the mean scores on enjoyment across different sports. As an extension of this figure, use *clustered* bar charts to break down further the enjoyment scores according to both sport and gender. In Dialog box 111, move *gender* into the *Other summary function* box. Click *OK*. For example, you can see that the mean scores on enjoyment for males and females who play football are 5.6 and 4.6 respectively (Figure 56).

The *Stacked* option of Dialog box 106 produces bar charts in which each category of a variable is represented by a separate bar. Furthermore, each bar is split into segments that represent the categories of a second variable. Figure 57 shows that for each sport played both by males and females, the top part of the bar represents the mean enjoyment score for males and the bottom part represents the mean score for females.

To create the *stacked* bar chart, in Dialog box 112 move *enjoyment* into the *other summary function* box, *activity* into the *category axis* box, and *gender* into the *define stacks by* box.

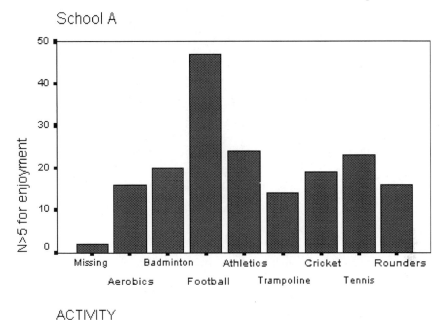

Figure 53

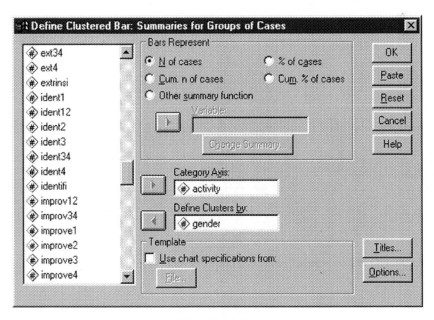

Dialog box 111

Sports practised by study participants

School A

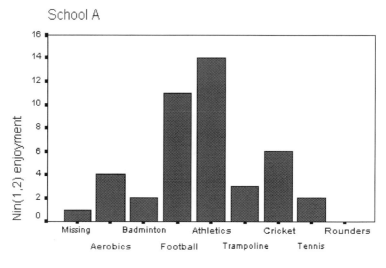

Figure 54

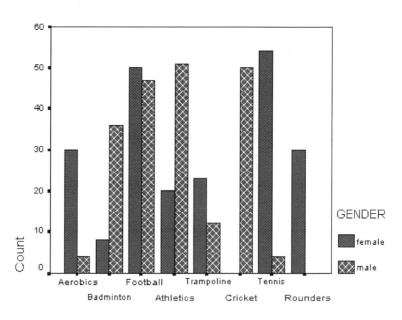

Figure 55

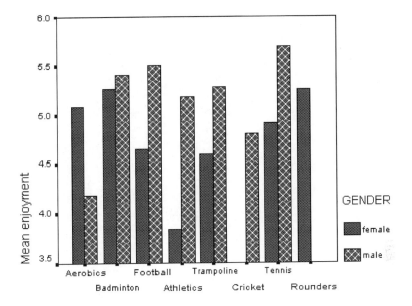

Figure 56

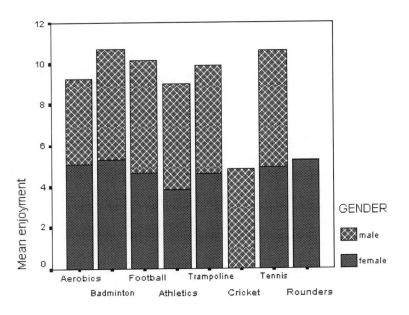

Figure 57

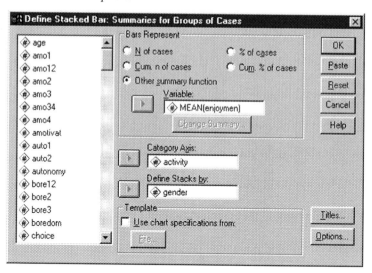

Dialog box 112

Summaries of separate variables (see Dialog box 106)
This option creates bar charts for different variables rather than for the different categories of a variable. Click *Simple* in Dialog box 106. Suppose you want to plot a bar chart with the mean scores of three different variables: effort, boredom, and enjoyment. Select these variables and move them into the *Bars Represent* box. Click *OK* (Dialog box 113).

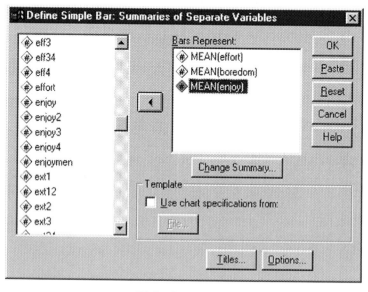

Dialog box 113

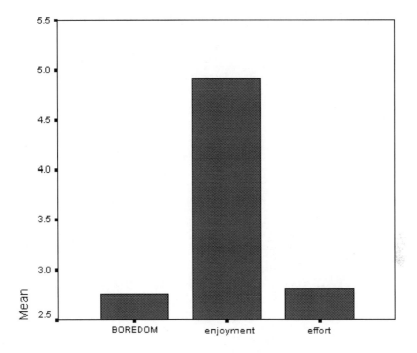

Figure 58

As you can see, the mean score on enjoyment is much higher than the mean scores on effort and boredom (Figure 58).

To find out the mean scores for males and females in each of the three variables, go to Dialog box 106 and select *Clustered*. Move *enjoy*, *effort*, and *boredom* into the *Bars represent* box. Move *gender* in the *Category Axis*. Click *OK* (Dialog box 114).

As you can see, some gender differences and similarities appear. For females, the highest mean score is on enjoyment and the lowest on boredom. For males, the highest mean score is also on enjoyment, but the lowest mean score is on effort (Figure 59).

Using a similar procedure, the *stacked* version (see Dialog box 106) of Figure 59 will look like Figure 60.

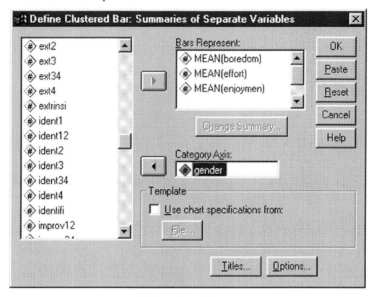

Dialog box 114

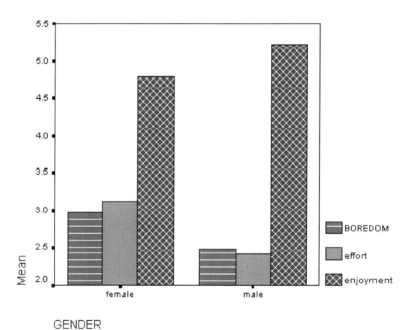

Figure 59

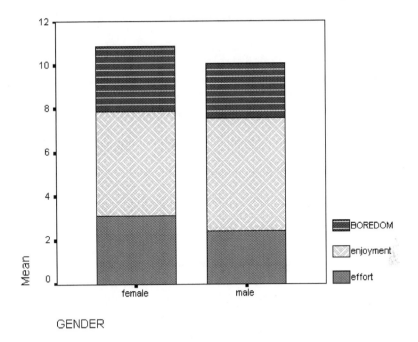

Figure 60

Values of individual cases (see Dialog box 106)
This option creates bars for each individual case of one or more variables. Obviously, this chart is not useful when the data file has a large number of cases. However, it can be informative when the sample size is small. Click *Simple* in Dialog box 106. Suppose you have a sample of 10 runners and you want to plot their lactate values after 30 minutes of running at the maximal lactate steady state intensity score. Move the *lact30* variable into the *Bars Represent* box. Click *OK* (Dialog box 115).

Figure 61 shows the lactate values of every single individual runner.

In Figure 61, the 10 athletes were identified by their case number. However, you can also identify them by their age or gender. In Dialog box 115, move *gender* into the *Category Labels/Variable* box. Click *OK*. Figure 62 is similar to Figure 61, but it labels the runners according to their gender rather than their case numbers.

Similar figures can be produced for multiple variables. Select *Clustered* from Dialog box 106. Move the variables *lact15* and *lact0* in the *Bars Represent* box. These variables show the lactate values at the 15th minute and at rest. Label the participants according to their *gender* and click *OK* (Dialog box 116).

Note that the bars represent the actual scores of every participant and not the mean scores of the two variables (Figure 63). Using a similar procedure, the same figure can be plotted as a *stacked* bar chart (Figure 64).

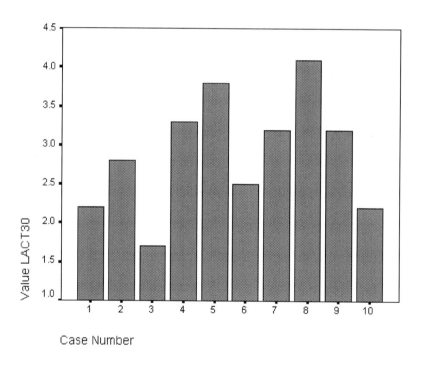

Dialog box 115

Figure 61

Line

This option has similar dialog boxes and outputs to those found in the *Bar* chart option. The main difference is that a line is used to connect the scores of different variables or the scores of different categories of a variable. Three

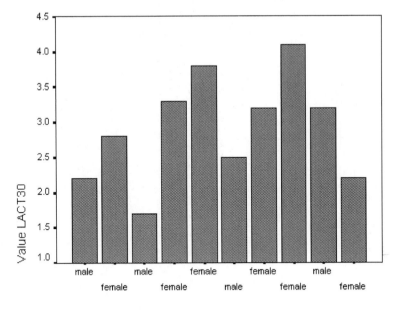

Figure 62

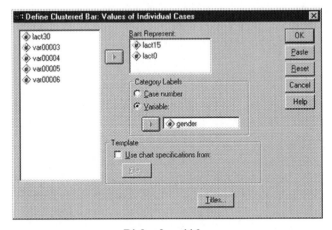

Dialog box 116

examples will be given here. For an explanation of the various options in the *Line* dialog boxes, see *Bar* chart above.

The first example is Figure 65 which is equivalent to Figure 52 (this time without a separate category for missing values). It shows a *simple* line chart of the enjoyment scores for different sports, with data being *the summaries for group cases*.

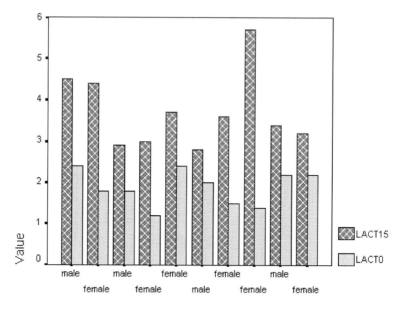

Figure 63

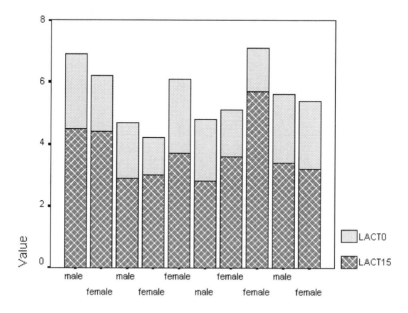

Figure 64

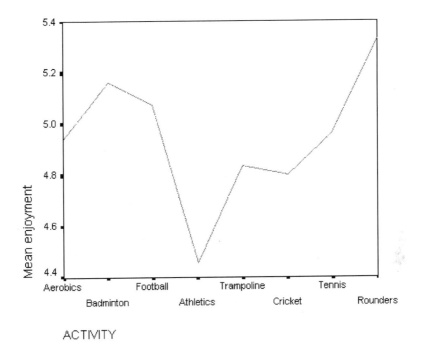

Figure 65

The second example is Figure 66. It shows a *multiple* line chart of the mean scores on enjoyment and boredom for different sports, with data being *summaries of separate variables*.

The third example is Figure 67. It shows a *drop-line* line chart of the lactate values of 10 participants at rest and after 15 minutes running on a maximal lactate steady state intensity score, with data being *values of individual cases*.

Note that in contrast to the previous two figures, Figure 67 shows individual and not mean (group) scores.

Area

Similar to *line* charts, SPSS can draw a line that connects the scores of different variables or the scores of different categories of a variable. In addition, the area between the line and the horizontal *x* axis is shadowed. The dialog boxes for *area* charts are similar to those used for *bar* and *line* charts. Figure 68 shows how Figure 65 appears when plotted as a *simple area* chart, with data being *summaries for group of cases*.

Figure 69 shows a *stacked* area chart with data representing *summaries of separate variables*. Each variable has its own shaded area, one at the top of the other. This figure is similar to Figure 66.

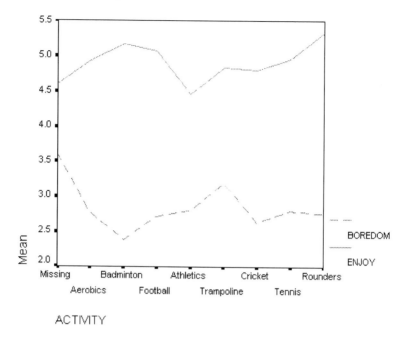

Figure 66

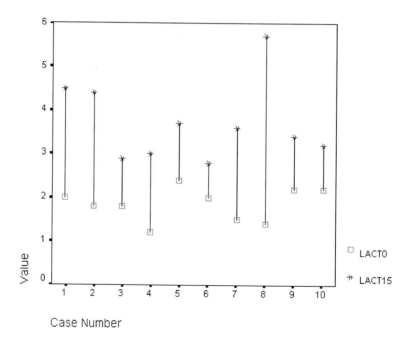

Figure 67

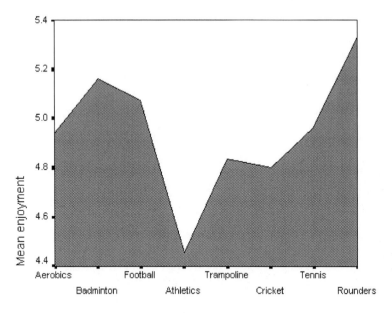

Figure 68

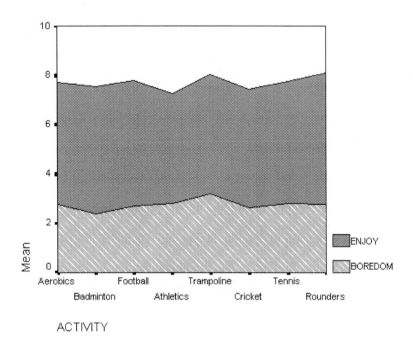

Figure 69

Pie

This is one of the most commonly used types of chart. The dialog boxes are similar to those presented above for *bar* charts. The slices of each pie can represent different categories of a variable or different variables. Figure 70 shows an example of a pie chart that describes the competitive level of a group of pupils (*summaries for group of cases*).

In order to show the percentages or the values of each slice, double click to edit the chart. Select *Options* from the *Chart* menu. At the top of Dialog box 117 you can arrange the orientation of the first slice. You can also specify a percentage value to be the minimum threshold for depicting a variable in a separate slice; all variables below this specified value will be considered too small and will be combined (*collapsed*) into an *Others* slice. *Text* under *Labels* gives names to the slices. You can also ask for the *values* and *percentages* of the slices. Select *Edit Text* to change the *labels* of the slices. Click *Format*.

In Dialog box 118 you can specify whether the labels should be *positioned inside* or *outside* the pie. For labels positioned outside the pie, *connecting line for outside labels* connects the labels with their respective slices. *Arrowhead on line* connects the labels with their respective percentages/values. In Dialog box 118, you can also ask for *frames* around the labels and customise the appearance of the *values* in the slices. If you want to keep the slices separated from each

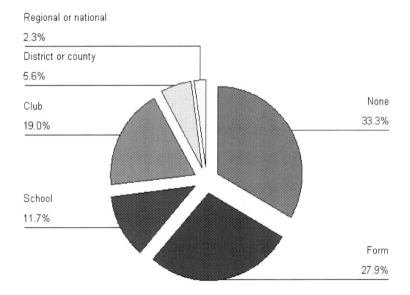

Figure 70

Dialog box 117

Dialog box 118

other (as in Figure 70), select *Exploded* from the *Pie* option in the *Gallery* menu. If you want to detach only one slice from the others, click on this slice, and select *Explode slice* from the *Format* menu.

Pareto

This option uses bars to summarise in a descending order different variables or different categories of the same variable. *Simple* pareto charts plot the *counts* or *sums* of a case number, category, or variable. *Stacked* charts have the additional feature of splitting each bar into segments which represent different categories or variables.

Dialog box 119 is an example of a *simple* pareto chart in which data represent *counts or sums for groups of cases*. Suppose you want to present the competitive level of a group of pupils. Select *level* and move this variable into the *Category Axis* box. Select *Counts* under *Bars Represent*, because you want to display the number of pupils in each competitive level. Alternatively, you could display *the sums of a variable* (e.g., hours of training per week) for each competitive level.

Dialog box 119

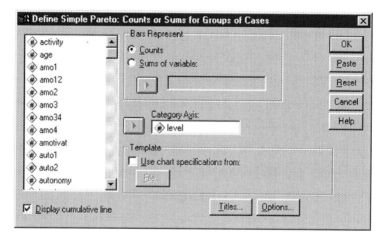

Dialog box 120

If you want to show the cumulative sum of the different competitive levels, select *Display cumulative line*. *Titles* and *Options* are similar to those described in other types of charts. Click *OK* (Dialog box 120). Figure 71 shows that 142 pupils do not play sport at a competitive level.

Sums of separate variables and *values of individual cases* in Dialog box 119 produce charts for different variables (e.g., strength, flexibility) and individual cases (pupils) respectively. A *stacked pareto chart* (see Dialog box 119) with data being *counts for groups of cases* is shown in Figure 72. It is similar to Figure 71, but it displays an additional breakdown of each competitive level into males and females. Move *level* into the *Category Axis* box and *gender* into the *Define Stacks by* box (Dialog box 121). Click *OK*.

Figure 72 shows that 84 females and 35 males are competing at form level. The gender breakdown is not shown for categories with a very small number of pupils.

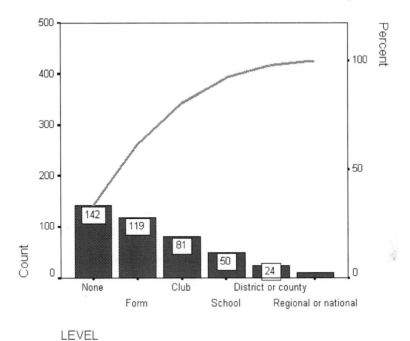

Figure 71

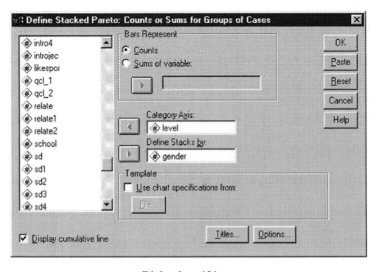

Dialog box 121

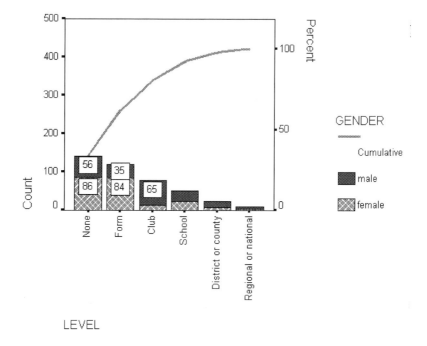

Figure 72

Boxplot

Boxplots can be requested either here or in the *Summarize/Explore* option of the *Analyze* menu. Boxplots show boxes which contain 50% of the cases for each variable or for each category of a variable.

Boxplots can be *simple* or *clustered* (see Dialog box 122). *Simple* boxplots have one box for each category or variable. *Clustered* boxplots contain clusters of boxes for each category or variable. These clusters are defined by a second variable.

Summaries for groups of cases summarise the categories of a variable within the categories of a second variable. For example, you can summarise boredom scores across different sports.

Move *boredom* into the *Variable* box and *activity* into the *Category Axis* box. If you want to use a variable name (e.g., year of study) to identify outliers, move this variable into the *Label Cases by* box. If this box is left empty, case numbers will be used instead to identify outliers. Click *OK* (Dialog box 123).

The boxplot is presented in Figure 73. The thick line in the middle of the box indicates the median of the boredom scores for each sport. The vertical lines extend to the highest and lowest boredom scores, leaving out the outlier. The circle at the top of the chart identifies the outlier.

Double click the chart to activate it. Select *Options* from the *Chart* menu. Here you can specify whether you want *outliers*, *case labels*, and the *counts for each category* to be displayed (Dialog box 124).

Dialog box 122

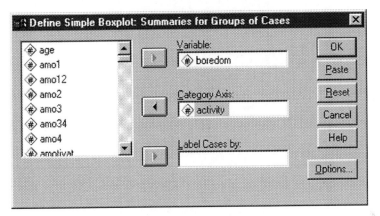

Dialog box 123

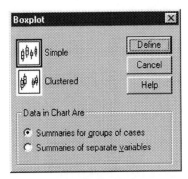

Dialog box 124

Figure 73 can also be plotted in a *clustered* form (see Dialog box 122). The clusters can be *defined*, for example, by the *gender* of the pupils (Dialog box 125).

Figure 74 illustrates this.

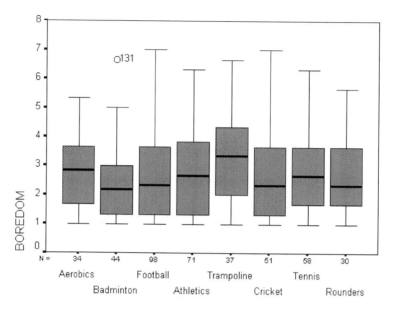

Figure 73

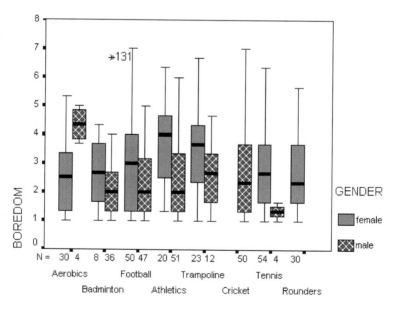

Figure 74

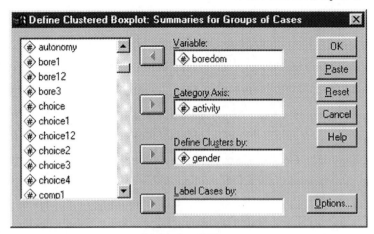

Dialog box 125

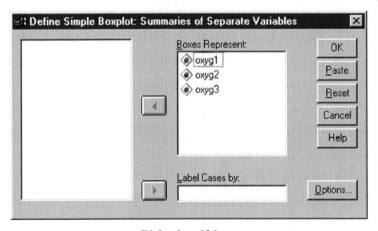

Dialog box 126

Summaries of separate variables in Dialog box 122 summarise two or more variables. Suppose you have measured the aerobic capacity of 8 rowers following three different testing protocols. Select *Simple* and click *Define*. Move the three variables (*oxyg1, oxyg2, oxyg3*) into the *Boxes Represent* box. Click *OK* (Dialog box 126).

Figure 75 illustrates the three variables.

You can also create a *clustered boxplot* which will cluster the same variables according to the values of a categorical variable. For this example, move *gender* into the *category axis*. *Label cases by* uses another variable (e.g., names of rowers) to provide labels for outliers. If this box is left empty, outliers are identified with their case number (Dialog box 127).

The *clustered boxplot* shown in Figure 76 clusters together the aerobic capacity values for each gender group.

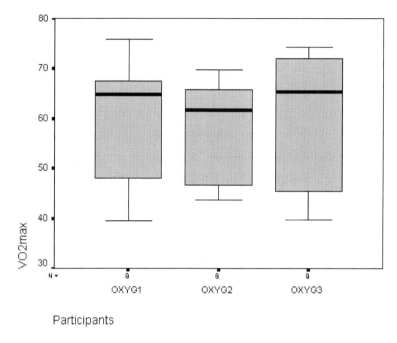

Figure 75

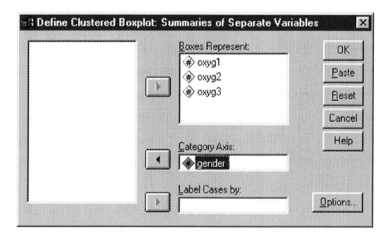

Dialog box 127

Error Bars

Error bars can *represent* the *confidence interval of the mean*, or the *standard error of the mean*, or the *standard deviation*. Similar to *boxplots*, error bars can be *simple* (i.e., have one bar per category of a variable) or *clustered* (i.e., have different bars for different variables (Dialog box 128)).

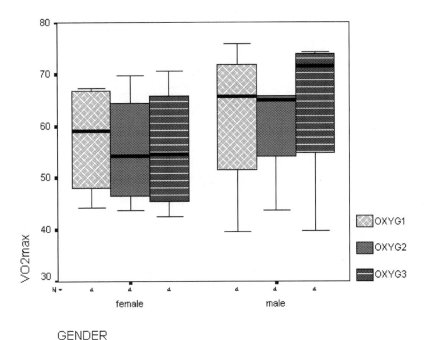

Figure 76

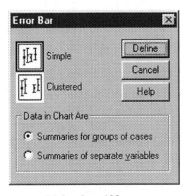

Dialog box 128

Here is an example of a *simple* error bar with data being *summaries for groups of cases*. This chart summarises the *confidence intervals* (default confidence *level* is *95%*) of javelin performance (distance in metres) of qualifiers and non-qualifiers for a major competition. If you want *bars to represent standard errors* or *standard deviations* you need to specify a *Multiplier*. The multiplier shows the number of standard errors or standard deviations above and below the mean represented by each error bar. For

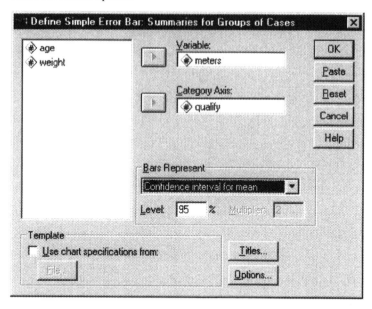

Dialog box 129

example, three standard deviations above and below the mean include around 99.7% of the sample. Finally, click *OK* (Dialog box 129).

Figure 77 illustrates the output showing the 95% confidence interval of the mean performance of qualifiers and non-qualifiers.

If you do not want the horizontal axis to display the counts for each category, double-click the chart to activate it, and remove the tick from *Display counts for categories* under *Options* in the *Chart* menu.

Summaries of separate variables in Dialog box 128 produce *simple* error bars for separate variables rather than for different levels of the same variable. Move *age* and *weight* in the *Error Bars* box of Dialog box 130. The bars will represent values which are 2 standard errors (i.e. *Multiplier* = 2) above and below the mean score of each variable. Click *OK*.

Figure 78 illustrates this.

Clustered error bars (see Dialog box 128) produce similar charts. In addition, you can specify a variable (e.g., gender) that can be used to cluster the error bars for each category or variable. For example, you can create one error bar for females and one for males separately for qualifiers and non-qualifiers (different categories of a variable), or separately for age and weight (different variables).

Scatter

Correlations between two or more variables can be presented graphically in a scatter plot. There are different types of scatter plots: simple, overlay, matrix and 3-D.

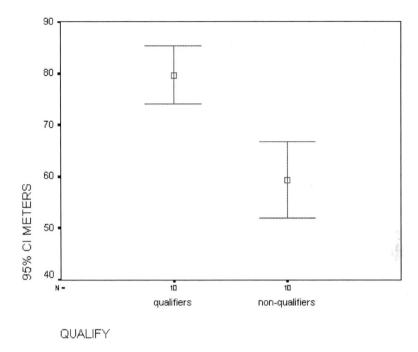

Figure 77

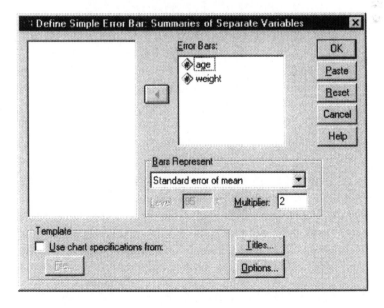

Dialog box 130

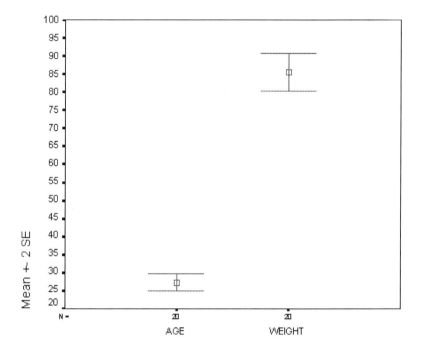

Figure 78

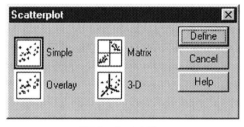

Dialog box 131

Simple

Simple scatter plots have two axes. Each participant is represented by a point that corresponds to the coordinates of his/her scores on the two variables (axes). Click *Define* (Dialog box 131).

In the example shown in Dialog box 132, the upper body muscle *strength* of 15 shot-putters is correlated with their personal performance record (*distance* in metres). Move *strength* and *distance* in the *Y* and *X* axes (or vice versa if you wish). *Set markers by* specifies a categorical variable (e.g., *country* of origin) which is used to distinguish the data points or markers. For example, different colours or different types of markers can be used for country A and country B. You may want to *label the cases* or data points using a third variable (e.g., the

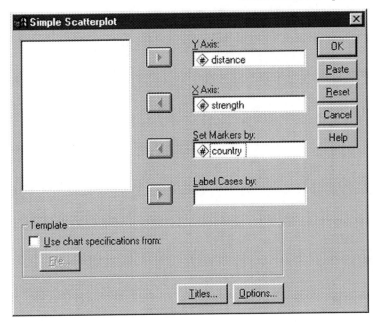

Dialog box 132

age of the shot-putters). With this option each case will have a label which will indicate the age of the shot-putters. If no variable is selected in this box, SPSS will use the case numbers to label the cases (as in Figure 79). Click *OK*.

The lines and numbers in Figure 79 are not normally displayed unless you double-click to activate the chart. Then, select *Options* from the *Chart* menu (Dialog box 133).

Show subgroups distinguishes the shot-putters from the two countries by using different colours or shapes of marker (in Figure 79, square for country A and circle for country B). Specify that you want the *case labels* to be *on*. Because the *label cases by* box in Dialog box 132 was left blank, the *cases* (athletes) are labelled by their *number* (i.e., 1–15). *Sunflowers* are used when no subgroups are specified (i.e., when the *set markers by* box in Dialog box 132 is left blank). *Sunflowers* are used in situations where two or more cases are overlapping. Each petal of the sunflower corresponds to one or more overlapping cases. Click on *Sunflowers Options* to specify the number of cases each petal will represent. In Figure 80 (taken from another data file which examined variable A and variable B), each petal represents one case. As you can see, there is a fair amount of overlap at the bottom left-hand corner.

Go back to Dialog box 133. *Fit Line* adds the best-fit line for the *total sample* as well as for each *subgroup* (i.e., country A and country B). This line represents the best linear estimate of the relationship between *strength and distance*. In Figure 79, the best-fit line for the total sample is the line with the positive slope. There are various *Fit Options* for the best-fit line. One of them is linear (*Linear*

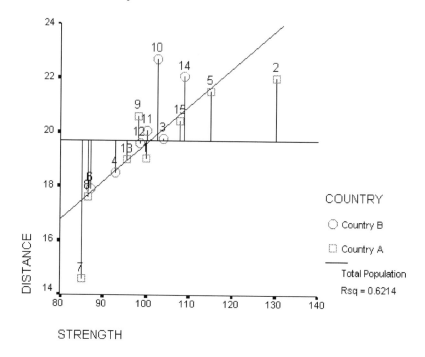

Figure 79

Dialog box 133

Regression), whereas the others are curvilinear. *Regression Prediction Line(s)* show the 95% confidence intervals of the regression line. *Mean* shows the confidence intervals of the mean predicted responses and *Individual* shows the confidence intervals of each case. Tick the *Regression Options* (to *include a*

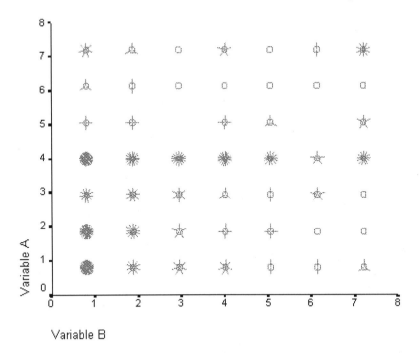

Figure 80

Dialog box 134

constant term in the regression equation) and the *display the R square* statistic (Dialog box 134).

Figure 81 is an example of a *Linear Regression Fit Method* showing the *95% confidence intervals* (top and bottom lines) of the mean predicted responses (middle line).

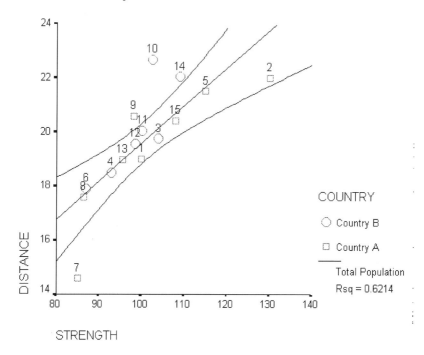

Figure 81

Go back to Dialog box 133. *Mean of Y Reference Line* draws a horizontal line parallel to the category (horizontal) axis. As you can see in Figure 79, the starting point of the reference line in the Y axis is the mean score of the *distance* variable ($M = 19.67$ m). The vertical lines represent the distance of each individual marker from the reference line (*Display spikes to lines*). Reference lines and vertical lines can be displayed for the *total* sample and/or for each *subgroup*.

Overlay
Overlay in Dialog box 131 is an extension of a *simple* scatter plot. It displays in the same chart the scatter plots of two or more pairs of variables. In Dialog box 135, select two variables and move them into the *Y-X Pairs* box. The first variable will be variable Y of the pair and the second variable will be variable X. Repeat this process for as many pairs as you would like to plot. If you want to swap the order of the variables in the pair click *Swap Pair*. A variable can be included in more than one pair. In the example shown in Dialog box 135, a scatter plot is shown for two pairs. The first pair consists of the variables of autonomy in P.E. classes and levels of enjoyment reported by pupils, and the second pair consists of the variables of boredom with P.E. and levels of effort exerted by pupils. Click *OK*.

Figure 82 uses square markers for the boredom-effort scatter plot, and circular markers for the autonomy-enjoyment scatter plot. Double-click to

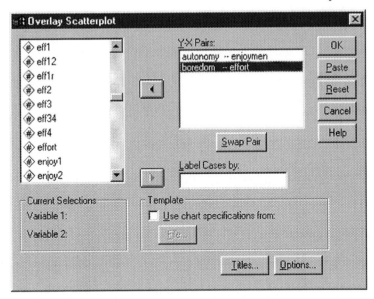

Dialog box 135

activate the chart. Select *Options* from the *Chart* menu. Ask to *display the fit line for each pair*. Figure 82 shows that there is a relatively small degree of overlap between the markers of the two plots.

Matrix
Matrix in Dialog box 131 displays the scatter plots for all possible combinations of two or more selected variables. Select three variables and move them into the *Matrix Variables* box. Choose *gender* to distinguish the markers of each scatter plot. Click *OK* (Dialog box 136).

Figure 83 presents the scatter plots for all possible combinations of the three variables. The number of rows and columns in the matrix is equal to the number of variables selected. Every variable in each pair has been plotted both as variable X and as variable Y (e.g., boredom-effort as well as effort-boredom). In each pair, males are represented with a circular marker and females with a square marker. To display the *line of best fit*, double click the chart and select *Options* from the *Chart* menu.

3-D in Dialog box 131 creates three-dimensional scatter plots. Let us see how the variables above (*enjoyment, effort*, and *boredom*) will be displayed into a *3-D* scatter plot. Move them into the *Y*, *X*, and *Z* axes, and set a *marker variable* if necessary (e.g., *gender*). Click *OK* (Dialog box 137).

The three-dimensional scatter plot is shown in Figure 84.

Double-click the chart to activate it. Select *Options* from the *Chart* menu. The options at the top of Dialog box 138 have been explained before (see *simple* scatter plot). *Spikes* are lines from each scatter point to the *floor, origin,* or *centroid* of all points. *Spikes* can help your orientation when rotating or printing

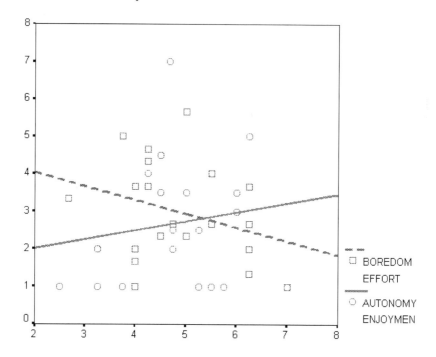

Figure 82

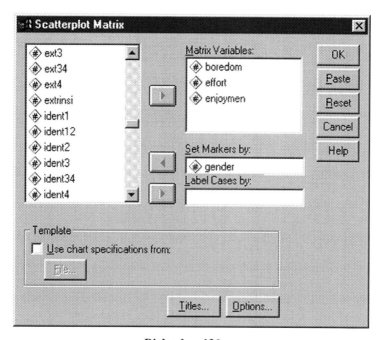

Dialog box 136

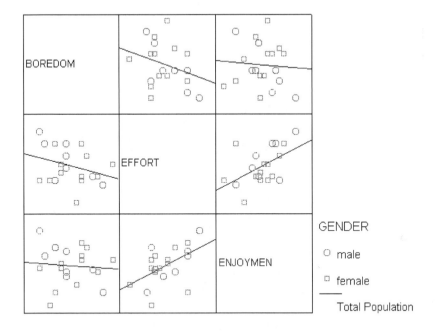

Figure 83

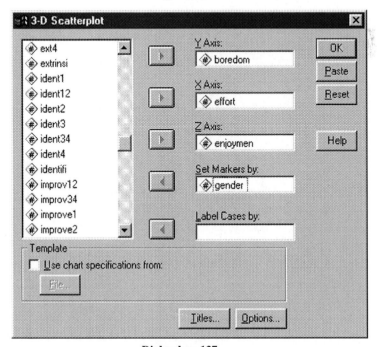

Dialog box 137

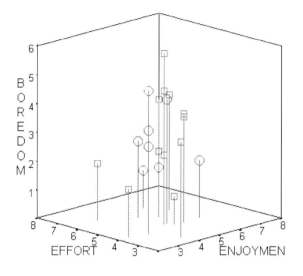

Figure 84

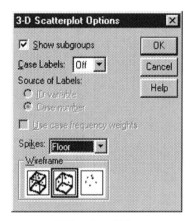

Dialog box 138

3-D scatter plots. With *Wireframe* you can choose whether you want to display 12, 9, or no edges around the scatter plot. Figure 84 has 9 edges.

For the rotation of *3-D* scatter plots, it is also worth looking at the *3-D rotation* option in the *Format* menu.

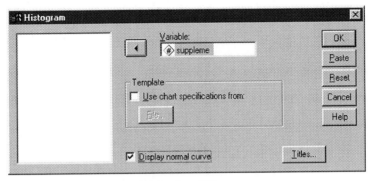

Dialog box 139

Histogram

Histograms can be requested either here or in the *Summarize frequencies* option of the *Analyze* menu. The histogram in Dialog box 139 presents data obtained from measuring the extent to which rowers believe that fluid supplement A can enhance their performance (1 = not at all, 5 = very much so). Click *Titles* to give a *title*, *subtitle*, or *footnote* to the chart. If you want to check whether the supplement (*suppleme*) scores have a normal distribution, tick the *Display normal curve* box. This produces Figure 85.

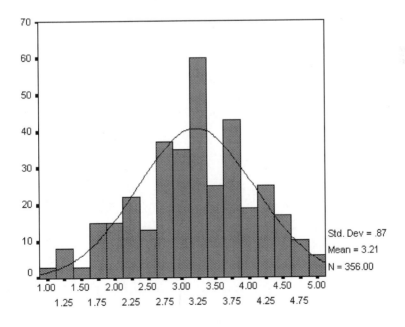

Figure 85

If you do not want SPSS to display descriptive statistics next to the chart, double click to activate it, and remove the tick from *Statistics in Legend* under *Options* in the *Chart* menu.

All chart options explained in the following pages are available in the *Chart Editor* only.

Gallery

Here you can convert an existing chart into another type of chart that is available from the list.

Chart

Options

At the bottom of Dialog box 140 you can convert an existing *simple* bar chart into a *clustered* or *stacked* bar chart.

The *change scale to 100%* option converts *clustered* bar charts into *stacked* bar chars and presents the percentages of the different categories or variables in the *stacked* chart. For example, with this option Figure 59 will be converted into Figure 86.

There are two *Line Options* in Dialog box 140. The first one, *connect markers with categories*, connects the markers of the same category that appear in different lines. For example, with this option Figure 66 will look like Figure 87.

As may be seen, the vertical lines connect the scores of each gender group on *enjoyment, effort,* and *boredom*.

The second *line option* is *display projection*. With this option you can specify the projection category of a variable. For example, you may want to specify a projection category for *boredom*. Click *Location* in Dialog box 140. Select a value (e.g., 4) and tick the *display reference line at location* option (Dialog box 141).

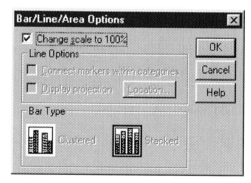

Dialog box 140

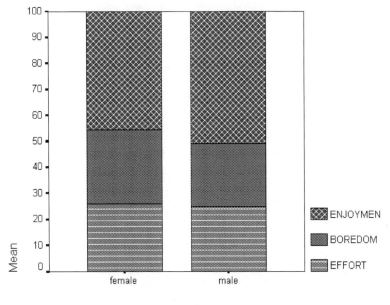

Figure 86

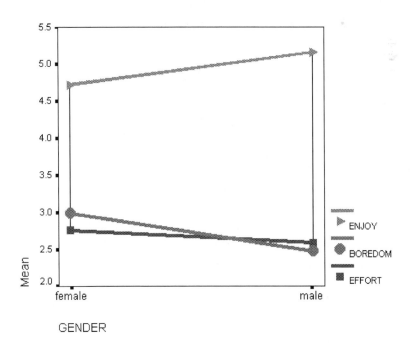

Figure 87

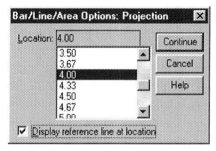

Dialog box 141

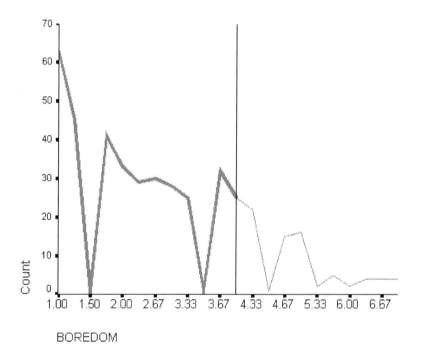

Figure 88

The chart will differentiate the categories to the right of the projected category with a thinner line style, and will display a vertical reference line on the fourth category (Figure 88).

Axis

Most two-dimensional charts have a *scale axis* and a *category axis*. A *scale axis* contains the scaled numerical values of a variable (e.g., percentages). Bar charts and line charts have one scale axis whereas scatter plots have two axes. A

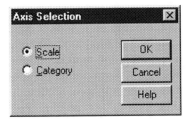

Dialog box 142

category axis has labels (e.g., names of athletes) or numeric values which are not necessarily scaled (e.g., numeric codes for different sports). Scatter plots and histograms do not have a category axis. Select *scale axis* in Dialog box 142 and click *OK*.

If you want the scale axis to be displayed in the chart, click *Display axis line* at the top of Dialog box 143. In the same dialog box you can specify the *title* of the axis and the *justification* of its text. Usually, SPSS shows the *minimum* and *maximum* values of the data in the scale axis. However, if you want to display a different data range, type the new minimum and maximum values in the *Displayed* boxes. You can also alter the *major increments* and *minor increments* of the data. Major increments determine the intervals of the axis (e.g., 0.5, 1, 1.5, 2, etc.) and should be given a number which splits the data range evenly. Minor increments determine the intervals within one major increment (e.g., 1.1, 1.2, 1.3, 1.4, 1.5) and, similarly, should be given a number which splits the data range evenly.

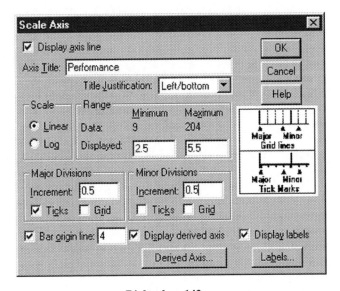

Dialog box 143

With *Display Derived Axis* you can ask for another axis (derived axis) which has a different data range from the scale axis. Click *Derived Axis*. Under *Definition* in Dialog box 144 you can specify the ratio of units between the scale axis and the derived axis. Suppose the variable in the scale axis represents different levels of performance and the variable in the derived axis represents the amount of money that corresponds to the different levels of performance. If the ratio is 1:2, a performance level of 1 will correspond to £2,000 and a performance level of 4 to £8,000. *Match* allows you to determine how the old and new values will match up. In this example, a performance level of 0 will correspond to £0.

In Dialog box 144 you can also specify the title of the derived *axis* and its *major* and *minor* increments, as well as the *Labels* of this axis and their properties. For example, you can assign a *leading character* (e.g., the sterling sign) or a *trailing character* (e.g., the percentage sign) to the labels. *Scaling factor* specifies the way the values in the derived axis are displayed. If you type *0.001*, the values will be 1000 times (i.e., 1/0.001) larger than the corresponding values in the data file. That is, a value of 3 in the data file, will appear as £3,000 in the derived axis. *Bar origin line* in Dialog box 143 specifies a value (e.g., 4) which is used as a reference point. Categories with values greater than 4 will have bars facing upwards and categories with values smaller than 4 will have bars facing downwards (see Figure 89).

In Dialog box 143 you can also specify the labels of the scale axis. The options under *Labels* are similar to the ones in Dialog box 144.

In Dialog box 142 click *Category*. Here you can provide the title and the labels of the horizontal axis of Figure 89.

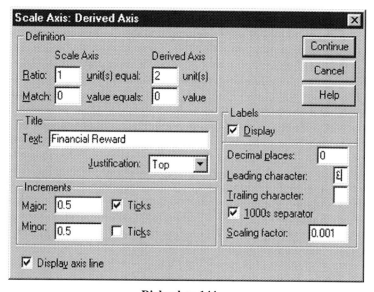

Dialog box 144

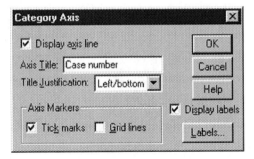

Dialog box 145

Dialog box 146

Click *Labels* in Dialog box 145. Use this option to indicate whether you want all labels to appear in the category axis, or, if there are too many, to display some of them only. In the example above (Dialog box 146), only half of the labels are shown and the ones that have been omitted are *marked with a tick*. Under *Labels* in Dialog box 146 you can change the labels of the categories in the axis. For example, instead of using the label '1', you can use the name of an athlete. The *orientation* of the labels (i.e., their position relative to the axis) can be *horizontal, diagonal, vertical*, or *staggered*.

The chart will look like Figure 89.

Bar Spacing (Dialog box 147)

This option is used in charts which display bars. *Bar margin* specifies the distance between the inner frame of the chart and the first and last bar. *Inter bar spacing* arranges the distance between the bars of the same cluster. Lastly, *inter-cluster spacing* specifies the distance between two or more clusters of bars.

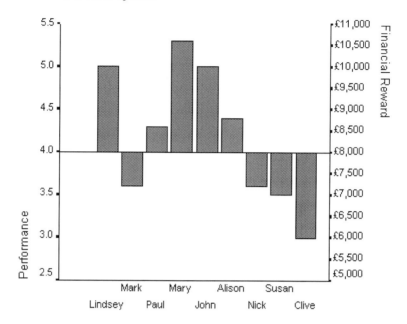

Figure 89

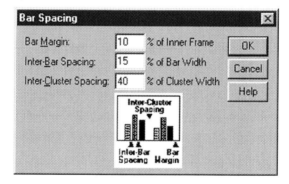

Dialog box 147

Title, Footnote, Legend

With these options you can modify the labels and the text orientation of the title,
subtitle, footnote, and legend of a chart.

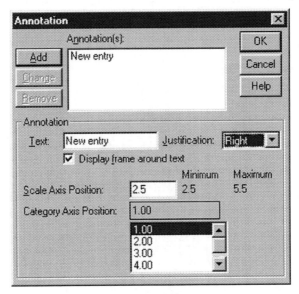

Dialog box 148

Annotation

This option allows you to add a short comment to one or more categories/ variables of a chart. For example, you may want to emphasise that athlete No1 is a new entry in the list. Type this comment in the *Annotation Text* box and tick *Display frame around text*. Click *Add*. Repeat this procedure to create as many annotations as you need and when you finish click *OK* (Dialog box 148).

Figure 90 shows the chart with the annotated text ('New entry') at the bottom left-hand side.

Reference Line

This line highlights a particular value in the scale axis or category axis. In the scale axis dialog box, specify a value between the minimum and the maximum values of the data and click *Add*. For example, you may want to create a line to separate those participants with a performance score below and above 4 (Dialog box 149).

Similarly, in the category axis dialog box, create a reference line to separate, for example, the first three athletes from the rest of the sample. Click *OK*. Figure 91 illustrates the result.

Outer Frame, Inner Frame

The difference between the two frames is that the inner frame covers the plot area only, whereas the outer frame covers the whole chart including its headings, footnotes, and legends.

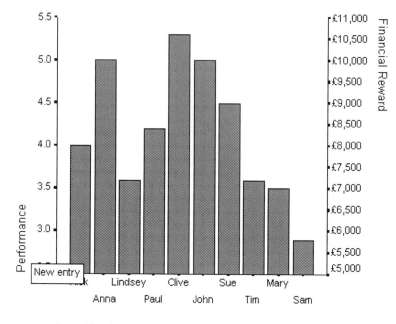

Figure 90

Dialog box 149

Refresh

Select this option if a chart is not displayed properly. This happens occasionally when you change the size of the chart window.

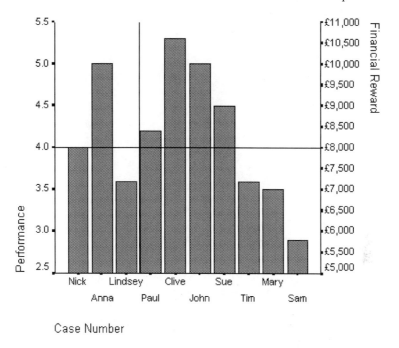

Figure 91

Series

Displayed

This option is useful when you want to modify an existing chart or convert it into another type. Take the example of Figure 59. Suppose you want to convert it from a *clustered bar chart* to a *multiple line chart*. At the top of Dialog box 150 decide which of the three variables (*enjoyment, effort, boredom*) will be included in the new chart. Indicate that you want to display the data for each variable in a *Line* format. Move the variables you do not want to include in the new chart into the *Omit* box. Follow the same procedure with the *category axis*.

The chart will look like Figure 92.

Transpose Data

This option moves the variables of the legend to the category axis and vice versa. Take the example of Figure 59. The variables in the category axis are *females* and *males*, and the legend variables are *enjoyment, effort*, and *boredom*. Using this option, the data in Figure 59 will be transposed, so that *females* and *males* will move to the legend and *enjoyment, effort*, and *boredom* will be moved to the category axis (Figure 93). This option is not the same with the *swapping axes* option (see *Format* menu below).

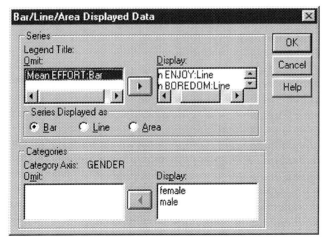

Dialog box 150

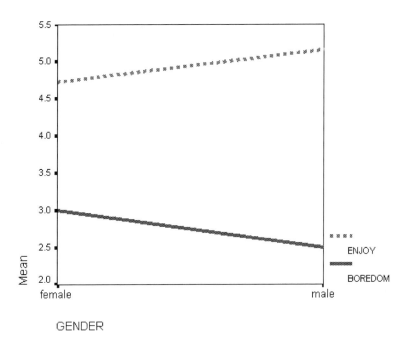

Figure 92

Format

Fill Pattern

If a chart has multiple variables plotted in bars, shaded areas, or pie slices, and you do not have a colour printer, you need to make sure that the different

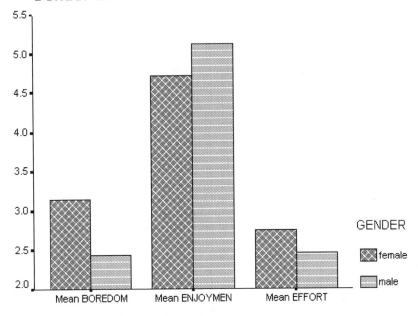

Figure 93

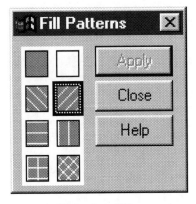

Dialog box 151

variables are clearly marked with different fill patterns (for an example, see Figure 93). To activate Dialog box 151, click on any of the variables in the chart and select one of the patterns from the dialog box. Then, click *Apply*. Note that different fill patterns can be applied to different variables only and not to different categories of the same variable.

Colors

Use this option to alter the colours of chart objects (bars, lines, areas, or pie slices). Click on a chart object first to activate this option. For example, in Figure 93 *fill* refers to the inside of the bars and *border* refers to the lines around the bar edges. To set a background colour, select *Inner* or *Outer Frame* (or both) from the *Chart* menu and then click with the mouse on the actual frames to activate Dialog box 152. Choose a background colour and click *Apply*. Click *Edit* for a larger variety of colours.

Markers

Markers are very useful when working with line charts. They can help you to distinguish the lines of different variables, especially if the chart is not printed on a colour printer. For an example of a line chart with markers, see Figure 92. To activate Dialog box 153 click on any of the lines in the chart. You can change both the *style* and the *size* of the line. The *Apply All* button applies a particular style and size to all the lines in the chart without closing the dialog box. The *Apply* button applies a particular style and size only to the selected line and closes the dialog box. The *Apply style* and *Apply size* buttons apply a particular style or size to a line without closing the dialog box.

Sometimes, you may notice that the *Apply* button is not activated. In order to activate it, go to the *Interpolation* option and select *display markers*.

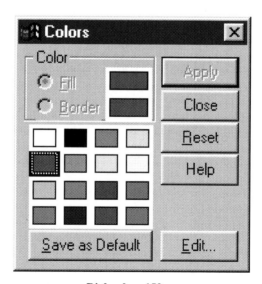

Dialog box 152

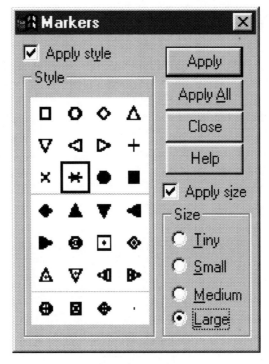

Dialog box 153

Line Style

With this option you can change both the *style* and the *weight* of a selected line in a chart. Make your choices and click *Apply*. You can also change the line *style* and *weight* (thickness) of a chart's axes, as well as its outer and inner frames. Remember that you need to click on the selected objects to activate Dialog box 154.

Bar Style

This option can be used with bar charts but not with histograms. You can add a *drop shadow* to the bars, or a *3-D effect*. Positive numbers in the *Depth* box apply the 3-D effect to the right of the bars whereas negative numbers apply the effect to the left. The *Apply All* button is convenient when you want to experiment with different bar styles, because it changes the bar style without closing the dialog box. In this way, you can try out different styles without having to open repeatedly Dialog box 155. *Close* applies the changes and closes the dialog box.

Figure 94 is an example of a 3-D bar chart with 50% depth.

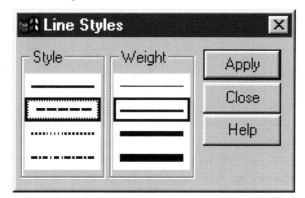

Dialog box 154

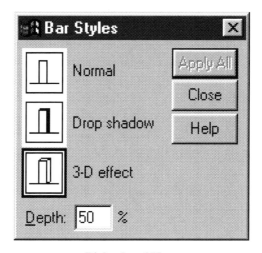

Dialog box 155

Bar Label Styles (Dialog box 156)

Use the *Standard* and *Framed* options to display the numeric values of bars. The *standard* option will display the values unframed. Frame the values to make them more visible when the colour or the fill pattern of a bar is dark.

Interpolation

With this option you can specify how data points should be connected in a line chart. To activate Dialog box 157, click on a line. *None* removes the lines from the chart, but the line markers will still appear if you select *Display markers* at the bottom of the dialog box. *Straight* connects data points with straight lines. The third style (*steps*) connects data points with horizontal lines. These lines are

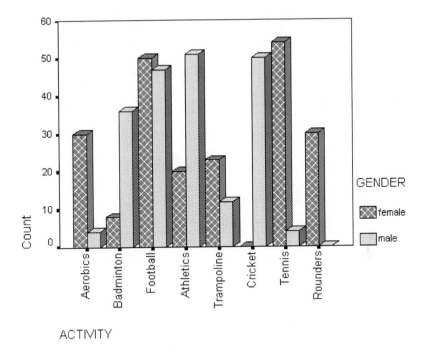

Figure 94

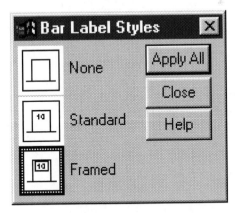

Dialog box 156

joined together with vertical lines. *Left, center,* or *right step,* specify whether the position of a data point on a horizontal line should be on the left, centre, or right of the line. The fourth style is very similar to the third style, but it does not display vertical lines. The fifth style connects data points with smooth lines. *Apply* implements a style only to the selected line, whereas *Apply All* applies a style to all lines.

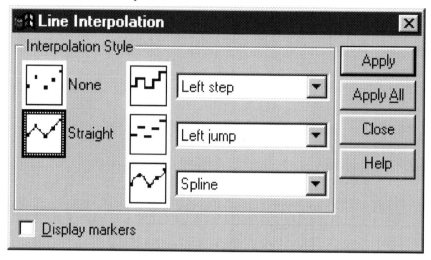

Dialog box 157

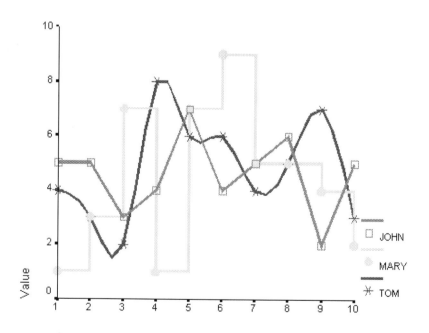

Figure 95

Figure 95 presents the performance of three athletes in ten different motor tasks. John's data points are connected with the second style (*straight line*), Mary's data points are connected with the third style (*Left step*), and Tom's data points are connected with the fifth style (*Spline*).

Text

Use this option to change the *font* type and *size* of the headings, footnotes, and legends.

3-D Rotation

With this option you can rotate a three-dimensional scatter plot. The buttons in the dialog box show the axes and the direction of the rotation. You can click on these buttons once or as many times as you wish, and then preview the outcome of the rotation in the middle of the dialog box. If you are not satisfied with the outcome, click *Reset* and the scatter plot will return to its original position. If you have chosen not to display the *wireframe* (see *3-D scatterplot* in the *Graphs* menu), none of the edges of the chart will be displayed. To facilitate your orientation, request from SPSS to *show the tripod*, that is, the three thick lines in the preview display of Dialog box 158. Click *Apply* to view the outcome of the rotation, and *Close* to close the dialog box when you are happy with the rotated chart.

Figure 96 is a 3-D rotated version of Figure 84.

Swap Axes

Use this option to swap axes in a two-dimensional chart so that the horizontal axis becomes the vertical axis and vice versa. This is not the same option with *transpose data* (in the *Series* menu). After swapping axes, Figure 95 will look like Figure 97.

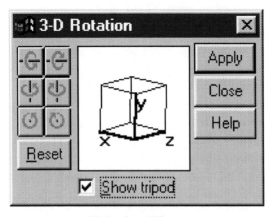

Dialog box 158

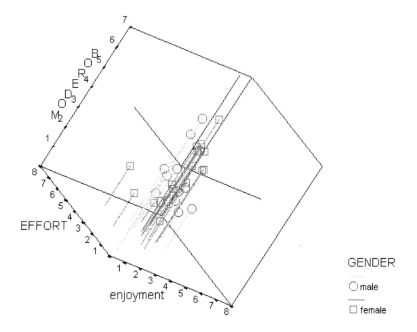

Figure 96

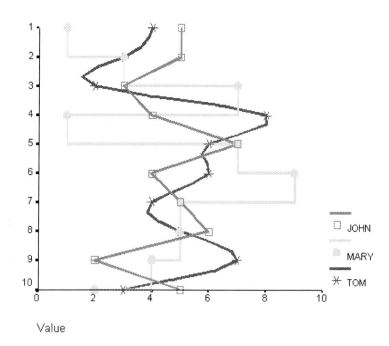

Value

Figure 97

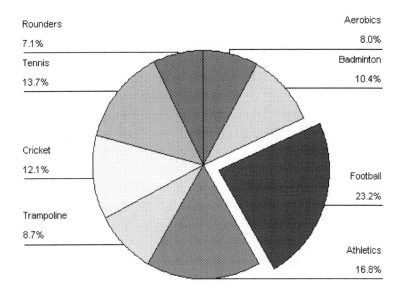

Figure 98

Explode Slice

Use this option in a pie chart to detach one or more slices from the rest. Click on the particular slices to activate this option. As you can see from Figure 98, the football slice has been 'exploded'. To 'explode' all slices, select *Pie* from the *Gallery* menu.

Break Line at Missing

Tick this option to indicate missing values by breaking a line in a line chart.

In Figure 99, Paul and Jean have been measured on seven different fitness tests, but both of them have missed some of the tests. Paul has missed tests 2 and 6, whereas Jean has missed tests 5 and 7.

Edit (SPSS tables)

When you double-click on SPSS tables to activate them some new menus and options appear (Figure 100).

Some of the options in the *Edit* menu, are similar to those described in Chapter 1. However, there are some unique options especially designed for editing SPSS tables.

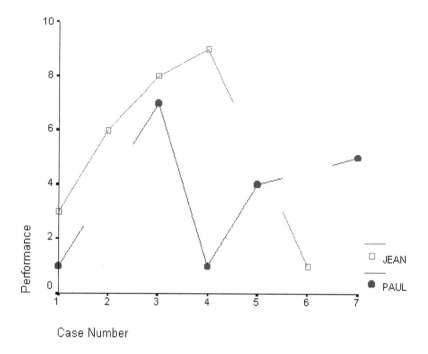

Figure 99

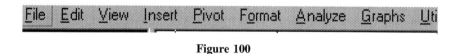

Figure 100

Select

With this option you can select and then edit different parts of a table (e.g., cells or labels). *Select Table* selects the entire table, whereas *Select Table Body* selects the cells and their labels leaving out the title and the footnotes. *Data cells* selects all cells in a row or column. To activate this option, click on the label of the particular row or column. *Data and label cells* activates both the cells and the labels of the particular row or column.

Group

Use this option to group multiple columns or rows. In Table 72, you may want to group the first four sports as being the 'most popular', and the last four sports as being the 'least popular'. To form the first group press the Shift button on the keyboard and, while pressing, click on the labels of the group. Repeat the same procedure with the second group.

Table 72

ACTIVITY

		Frequency	Percent	Valid Percent	Cumulative Percent
Valid	Football	98	22.9	23.2	23.2
	Athletics	71	16.6	16.8	40.0
	Tennis	58	13.6	13.7	53.7
	Cricket	51	11.9	12.1	65.7
	Badminton	44	10.3	10.4	76.1
	Trampoline	37	8.6	8.7	84.9
	Aerobics	34	7.9	8.0	92.9
	Rounders	30	7.0	7.1	100.0
	Total	423	98.8	100.0	
Missing	9.00	5	1.2		
Total		428	100.0		

Table 73

ACTIVITY

			Frequency	Percent	Valid Percent	Cumulative Percent
Valid	Group Label	Football	98	22.9	23.2	23.2
		Athletics	71	16.6	16.8	40.0
		Tennis	58	13.6	13.7	53.7
		Cricket	51	11.9	12.1	65.7
	Group Label	Badminton	44	10.3	10.4	76.1
		Trampoline	37	8.6	8.7	84.9
		Aerobics	34	7.9	8.0	92.9
		Rounders	30	7.0	7.1	100.0
	Total		423	98.8	100.0	
Missing	9.00		5	1.2		
Total			428	100.0		

Select the *group* option. Two group labels will appear in Table 73.

Double click to edit the *Group Labels*. Name the first group as 'most popular sports' and the second group as 'least popular sports' (Table 74).

Ungroup

Select this option to ungroup the variables of a group. Also, use this option before creating new groups if other groups already exist.

Table 74

ACTIVITY

			Frequency	Percent	Valid Percent	Cumulative Percent
Valid	Most popular sports	Football	98	22.9	23.2	23.2
		Athletics	71	16.6	16.8	40.0
		Tennis	58	13.6	13.7	53.7
		Cricket	51	11.9	12.1	65.7
	Least popular sports	Badminton	44	10.3	10.4	76.1
		Trampoline	37	8.6	8.7	84.9
		Aerobics	34	7.9	8.0	92.9
		Rounders	30	7.0	7.1	100.0
	Total		423	98.8	100.0	
Missing	9.00		5	1.2		
Total			428	100.0		

Drag to Copy

Use this option to copy the label (original label) of a row or column onto the label (destination label) of another row or column. Click on the original label. Drag it with the mouse and place it on the destination label. As you can see, the destination and the original labels become identical.

View

Hide

Select this option to hide a row or column. For example, you may want to hide the *Football* row of Table 72. First, select this row by using the *Select Data and Label cells* option of the *Edit* menu. Then use the *Hide* option. To show again the *Football* row select *Show all categories* (see below).

Hide/Show Dimension Label

You can hide or show the label of a dimension. For example, Table 72 has two dimension labels: *activity* and *statistics* but only the former is visible. Click on one or both to hide them (or reveal them if they are hidden).

Show All Categories

This option shows all hidden categories (see *Hide* above). To activate it, click on any of the category labels.

Show All Footnotes

Use this option to display all the footnotes you have inserted (see *Insert footnote* below).

Show All

This option reveals all hidden parts of a table (i.e., dimension labels, categories, and footnotes).

Gridlines

Use this option to insert gridlines (i.e., cell borders). Note that gridlines are displayed but are not printed.

Insert

Title, Caption, Footnote

Use this option to give a title to a table. If a title has already been provided by SPSS, double-click the chart to edit that title. With this option you can also insert a caption at the bottom of a table. To insert one or more footnotes click first on the appropriate cells.

Pivot

Transpose Rows and Columns

With this option you can change the appearance of a table, so that rows become columns and vice versa. For example, using *transpose rows and columns* Table 72 will look like Table 75.

Move Layers to Rows

Layers were described before (see *Custom Tables* in the *Analyze* menu). The *General Table* (Table 76) shows the different types of sport practised by Year 9 and Year 10 pupils. The table has one layer (*gender*) which displays the results separately for females and males. Use the drop-down list to move from one gender group to the other.

The *Move layers to rows* option transfers the categories of a layer to the rows of a table. This means that each sport frequency is not presented separately for females and males (i.e., in different layers, as in Table 76), but it is combined in different rows of the same table (as in Table 77).

Table 75

ACTIVITY

| | Valid | | | | | | | | | Missing | Total |
	Football	Athletics	Tennis	Cricket	Badminton	Trampoline	Aerobics	Rounders	Total	9.00	Total
Frequency	98	71	58	51	44	37	34	30	423	5	428
Percent	22.9	16.6	13.6	11.9	10.3	8.6	7.9	7.0	98.8	1.2	100.0
Valid Percent	23.2	16.8	13.7	12.1	10.4	8.7	8.0	7.1	100.0		
Cumulative Percent	23.2	40.0	53.7	65.7	76.1	84.9	92.9	100.0			

Table 76

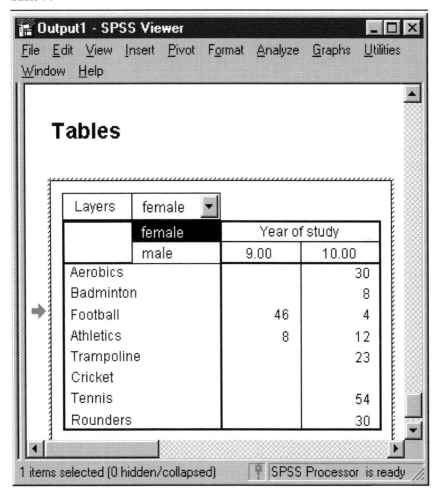

Move Layers to Columns

This option will move the categories of a layer (e.g., *males* and *females*) to the columns of the table. Table 78 differs from Table 77 in that each column presents separately the sport activities of each year group within each gender group.

Reset Pivots to Defaults

Use this option to undo any changes in the appearance of rows and columns and restore the original table settings.

Table 77

		Year of study	
		9.00	10.00
female	Aerobics		30
	Badminton		8
	Football	46	4
	Athletics	8	12
	Trampoline		23
	Cricket		
	Tennis		54
	Rounders		30
male	Aerobics		4
	Badminton		36
	Football	47	
	Athletics	12	39
	Trampoline		12
	Cricket		50
	Tennis		4
	Rounders		

Pivoting Trays

This option transposes rows and columns and moves categories from layers to rows and columns by rearranging the icons representing a row (bottom), a layer (left) and a column (right). For example, in order to move a category from a layer to a row, drag the layer icon next to the row icon (Figure 101).

Moving categories from layers to rows produces a table which, in contrast to Table 77, presents the gender breakdown separately for each sport (Table 79).

Go to Layer

Use this option to change the display of a table by viewing different layers or different categories of the same layer. In Dialog box 159, there are two layers: *gender* and competitive *level*. Select the category of a layer you want to display in the *Categories for Layers* box. To display different categories without leaving

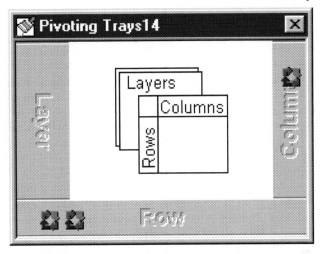

Figure 101

Table 78

	female		male	
	Year of study		Year of study	
	9.00	10.00	9.00	10.00
Aerobics		30		4
Badminton		8		36
Football	46	4	47	
Athletics	8	12	12	39
Trampoline		23		12
Cricket				50
Tennis		54		4
Rounders		30		

the dialog box, click *Apply*. To display a category and then exit the dialog box, click *OK*.

Format

Cell Properties (Dialog box 160)

Here you can specify the type and the properties of one or more table cells. Select these cells to activate this option. With the *Value* tab you can specify the type of variables in the cells (*number*, *date*, or other) and their *format*. If the

Table 79

		Year of study	
		9.00	10.00
Aerobics	female		30
	male		4
Badminton	female		8
	male		36
Football	female	46	4
	male	47	
Athletics	female	8	12
	male	12	39
Trampoline	female		23
	male		12
Cricket	female		
	male		50
Tennis	female		54
	male		4
Rounders	female		30
	male		

specified format exceeds the cell width, you can either change the width (see the *Margins* tab below) or ask SPSS to select a shorter format (*Adjust format for cell width*).

The *Alignment* tab arranges the horizontal and vertical alignment of the text as well as the alignment of numbers in the selected cells (Dialog box 161).

The *left, center,* and *right horizontal alignment* options align text and numbers left, centre, and right of the selected cells. *Mixed alignment* aligns numbers and dates at the right of the selected cells, and text at the left of the cells. *Decimal alignment* aligns decimal points at a specified offset from the right of the cells. *Top, center,* and *bottom alignment,* align variables at the top, centre, and bottom of the selected cells. The *Margins* tab lets you specify the *top, bottom, left,* and *right* margins of the cells. The *Shading* tab arranges the shading, *background* colour, and *foreground* colour of the selected cells. To change the colour of numbers, text, or dates in the cells use the *Font* option below.

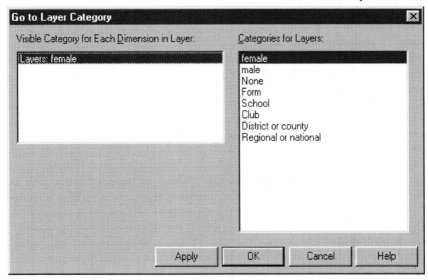

Dialog box 159

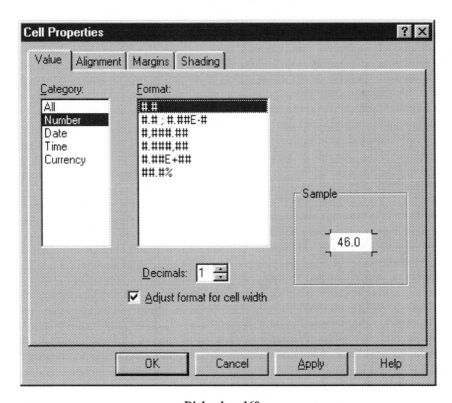

Dialog box 160

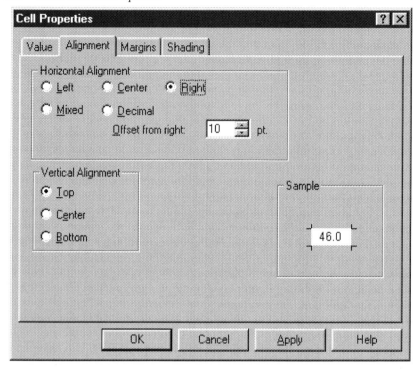

Dialog box 161

Table Properties (Dialog box 162)

Here you can specify the properties of a table. In the *General* tab, the *Hide empty rows and columns* option hides rows and columns which have no numbers, dates, or text. In this tab you can also identify the *minimum and maximum width for the labels* of the row and column cells. This is particularly useful when you have unusually long labels which do not fit in the pre-specified cell width.

In the *Footnotes* tab you can select whether the footnotes in a table should have an *alphabetic format* (i.e., a, b, c) or a *numeric format* (i.e., 1, 2, 3). You can also specify whether the marker of a footnote should be displayed above (*superscript*) or below (*subscript*) the text or number contained in a cell.

Cell Formats (see Dilaog box 163) specifies different cell formats for different *areas* of a table. Select the *area* you are interested in (e.g., *data, title, row labels, column labels*). You can specify the *text* size, type, and colour, the horizontal and vertical *alignment*, the *shading, foreground, background*, and *margins* for all the cells in the selected *area*. Use this option when you want to apply the same format to all the cells in the specified *area*. In contrast, use the *cell properties* option (in the *Format* menu) when you want to apply a particular format to certain cells in the specified *area*.

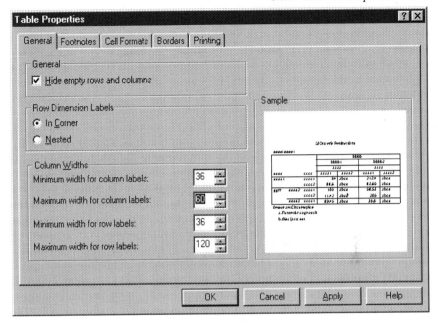

Dialog box 162

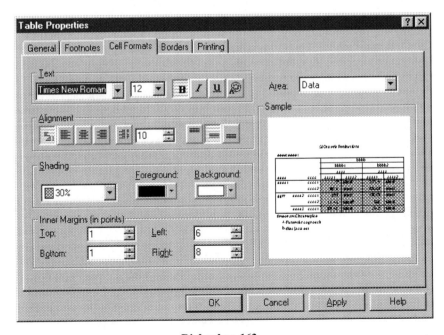

Dialog box 163

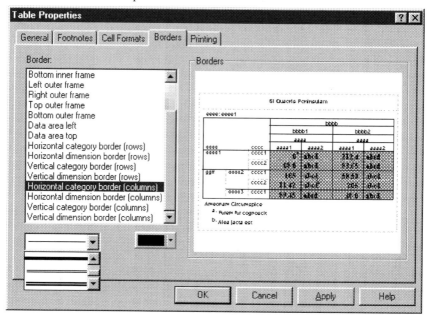

Dialog box 164

In the *Borders* tab select the borders that should be applied to different parts of a table. More than one table part (see *Border* box) can have the same border style. At the bottom of the dialog box choose the line and the colour of the borders (Dialog box 164).

Click the *Printing* tab (see Dialog box 165). Here you can indicate whether you want to print all layers as separate tables (*Print all layers*), or *print each layer on a separate page*. Ask SPSS to *rescale a wide and long table to fit the page*. This option makes sure that such a table is resized so that it can be printed on one page only. *Window/Orphan* lines specify the minimum number of rows and columns that should be printed on any page if a table is too wide or too long. For such tables, you can also indicate the *Position of continuation text* (i.e., 'cont.'). To view the continuation text, select *Print Preview* from the *File* menu.

TableLooks (Dialog box 166)

Use this option to change the appearance of tables.

A number of styles are available in the *TableLook Files* box. The *Academic* style is compatible with the table style recommended by the American Psychological Association. Some of the tables in this book are presented in this style. The *Reset all cell formats to the TableLook* option at the bottom left-hand side of the dialog box resets all edited cells back to the original cell format defined by the selected style. The styles can be changed and saved under

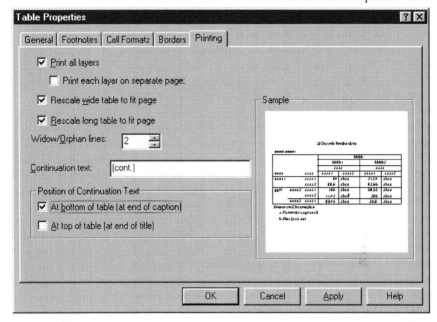

Dialog box 165

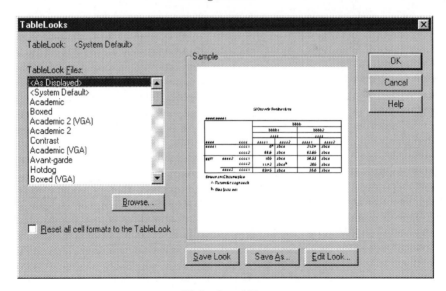

Dialog box 166

TableLook Files (use *Save Look*) or under a separate file/directory (use *Save As*). Click on *Edit Look* to modify the properties of a table. The *General, Footnotes, Cell Formats, Borders,* and *Printing* tabs are identical to those used in *Cell Properties and Table Properties* options (see *Format* menu above).

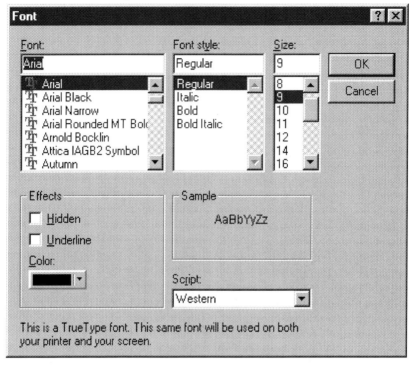

Dialog box 167

Font (Dialog box 167)

You can change the *size*, colour, type, and *style* of the text in one or more cells. Highlight these cells to activate the *Font* option. Note that you can hide the content of the cells by selecting *Hidden* under *Effects*.

Footnote Marker (Dialog box 168)

Use this to edit the format of a footnote marker. First, click on a footnote to activate this option. The *standard marker* can be either numeric or alphabetic depending on what you have chosen in the *Footnotes* tab of the *Table Properties*. Alternatively, you can specify your own *special marker*.

Set Data Cell Widths

Use this option to ensure that all data cells have the same width.

Renumber Footnotes

If you have modified some columns or rows, you may need to re-number their footnotes so that the numbers match up with the new columns or rows.

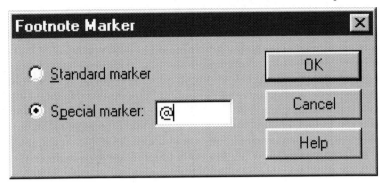

Dialog box 168

Rotate Inner Column Labels

With this option you can rotate the column labels as in Table 80.

Table 80

GENDER

		Frequency	Percent	Valid Percent	Cumulative Percent
Valid	female	218	50.9	51.4	51.4
	male	206	48.1	48.6	100.0
	Total	424	99.1	100.0	
Missing	9.00	4	.9		
Total		428	100.0		

5   Miscellaneous options

Utilities

Variables (Dialog box 169)

This is a very useful option because it provides summary information for all variables in a data file. Specifically, it displays the label, type, and measurement level of a variable, the code which indicates missing values, and the labels for the different values of a variable. Clicking on the *Go To* button will take you to the exact location of the variable in the data file, which can be quite handy if the data file is large.

File Info

This option also displays summary information for all variables in an output file. Note that this option can be used only for data files which are currently open. To display file information for stored files, select *Display Data Info* in the *File* menu.

Define Sets

In some cases, the data file contains a large number of variables. This can slow down the analysis, because every time you open a dialog box you have to locate and select the variables you want to analyse from a large variable list. To speed up this process, you can group some of the variables into sets which you can label with a specific name. After defining these sets, the dialog boxes will display only the sets and not the variables within each set. Highlight the variables you want to include in a set and move them into the *Variables in Set* box. At the top of the dialog box, label the set and click *Add set*. In the same way, you can create as many sets as you need. Note that one variable can belong to more than one set (Dialog box 170).

Use Sets (Dialog box 171)

With this option you can select the *sets* you want to use in subsequent analyses by moving them into the *Sets in Use* box.

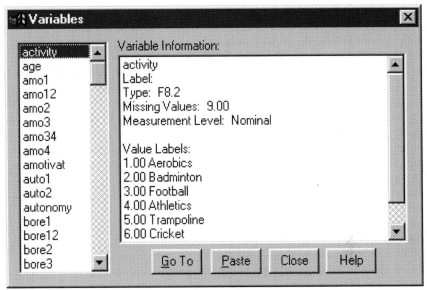

Dialog box 169

Run Script (Dialog box 172)

Scripts are groups of commands which can modify the appearance of tables in an output file. For example, the script *change sig to p =* changes the label that SPSS uses to indicate significance levels. In order to activate these scripts you need to select the appropriate table in the output file by clicking on it. Of course, the above script will not run if the table does not have a significance level column. After selecting the appropriate table, go to the *Run script* dialog box. Locate the file with the scripts in the SPSS folder (usually, it is within the Program Files folder). Then, select the relevant script and click *Run*.

To use autoscripts, see the relevant option in the *Edit* menu. If you want to create your own script, go to the *Open* menu and select *New script*. Creating a new script is not recommended for beginners. If, however, you decide to create a new one, you can transform it into an autoscript by going to *Option* in the *Edit* menu, and selecting the *Autoscript* Tab. Click on the *Browse* button and insert your new autoscript.

Menu Editor

This option enables you to create new options in a menu or even a new menu.

Run

Run is available only when you open a Syntax window. *All* will run all the commands that are currently written in the Syntax window. *Selection* will run

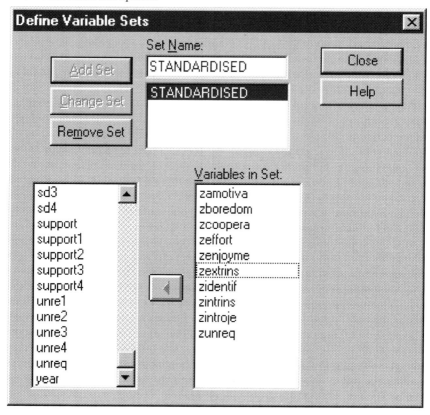

Dialog box 170

the commands you have selected by highlighting them. *Current* will run only the command upon which the cursor is placed. *To End* will run the commands placed between the cursor's position and the end of the window.

Window

This is a self-explanatory menu. Here you can minimise all open windows, or move from one open window to another.

Help

This menu is also self-explanatory. The *Topics, Tutorial*, and *Ask me* menus are there to provide answers to most of your questions. The *Statistics Coach* offers advice on what analysis or statistical tests are needed for your research purposes.

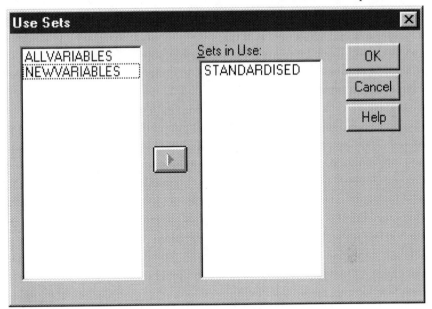

Dialog box 171

Insert

This menu is available only in an Output window.

Page Break/Clear Page Break

These options insert or delete a page break (divider). To activate these options, select the position in the output where you want to insert the page break. Use *Insert Break* to insert a page break before a long table so that the table can fit in one page and not break across two pages. If you decide to remove the page break, highlight the position in the output where it has been inserted and select *Clear Page Break*.

New Heading/New Title/New Text

These options give you the chance to provide more meaningful names to the various tables and charts in the output. Click on a table or chart to activate these options.

Insert Old Graph/Text File/Object

These options insert charts, text, or tables from an old output file into a new one. They are particularly useful when you want to pull together information from different output files.

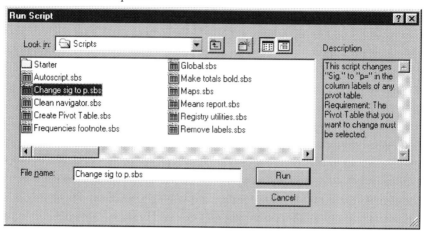

Dialog box 172

Format

This menu is available only in an Output window.

Align Left, Center, Right

Select the parts of the output you want to align, and use the *left*, *center*, or *right* alignment.

Suggested reading

Bartlett, R. (1997). The use and abuse of statistics in sport and exercise sciences. *Journal of Sports Sciences*, **15**, 1–2.

Bouffard, M. (1993). The perils of averaging data in adapted physical activity research. *Adapted Physical Activity Quarterly*, **10**, 371–391.

Cohen, J. (1992). A power primer. *Psychological Bulletin,* **112**, 155–159.

Cohen, J. and Cohen, P. (1983). *Applied Multiple Regression/Correlation Analysis for the Behavioural Sciences* (2nd edn.). Hillsdale, NJ: Lawrence Erlbaum.

Cohen, L. and Holliday, M. (1996). *Practical Statistics for Students: An Introductory Text.* Paul Chapman.

Duda, J. L. (ed.) (1998). *Advances in Sport and Exercise Psychology Measurement.* Morgantown, WV: Fitness Information Technology.

Feldt, L. S. and Ankenmann, R. D. (1998). Appropriate sample sizes for comparing alpha reliabilities. *American Psychological Measurement*, **22**, 170–178.

Hair, J. F., Anderson, R. E., Tatham, R. L. and Black, W. C. (1998). *Multivariate Data Analysis* (5th edn). Upper Saddle River, NJ: Prentice Hall.

Howell, D. C. (1997). *Statistical Methods for Psychology* (4th edn). Belmont, CA: Duxbury.

Kline, P. (1994). *An Easy Guide to Factor Analysis.* London: Routledge.

Kline, P. (2000). *The Handbook of Psychological Testing* (2nd edn). London: Routledge.

Lamb, K. (1998). Test-retest reliability in quantitative physical education research: A commentary. *European Physical Education Review*, **4**, 145–152.

Martens, R. (1987). Science, knowledge, and sport psychology. *The Sport Psychologist*, **1**, 29–55.

Nevill, A. (1996). Validity and measurement agreement in sports performance. *Journal of Sports Sciences*, **14**, 199.

Nevill, A. (2000). Just how confident are you when publishing the results of your research? *Journal of Sports Sciences*, **18**, 569–570.

Norusis, M. J. (1998). *SPSS® 8.0: Guide to Data Analysis.* Upper Saddle River, NJ: Prentice-Hall.

Pedhazur, E. J. and Schmelkin, L. (1991). *Measurement, Design, and Analysis: An Integrated Approach*. Hillsdale, NJ: Erlbaum.

Safrit, M. J. and Wood, T. M. (1989). *Measurement Concepts in Physical Education and Exercise science*. Champaign, IL: Human Kinetics.

Schmidt, F. L. (1996). Statistical significance testing and cumulative knowledge in psychology: Implications for training of researchers. *Psychological Methods*, **1**, 115–129.

Schutz, R. W. and Gessaroli, M. E. (1987). The analysis of repeated measures designs involving multiple dependent variables. *Research Quarterly for Exercise and Sport*, **58**, 132–149.

Schutz, R. W. and Gessaroli, M. E. (1993). Use, misuse, and disuse of psychometrics in sport psychology research. In R. N. Singer, M. Murphey and L. K. Tennant (Eds), *Handbook of Research on Sport Psychology* (pp. 901–917). New York: Macmillan.

Schwarz, N. (1999). Self-reports: How the questions shape the answers. *American Psychologist*, **54**, 93–105.

Stevens, J. (1999). *Applied Multivariate Statistics for the Social Sciences* (3rd edn). Hillsdale, NJ: Lawrence Erlbaum.

Tabachnick, B. G. and Fidell, L. S. (1996). *Using Multivariate Statistics* (3rd edn). New York: Harper Collins.

Thomas, J. R., Lochbaum, M. R., Landers, D. M. and He, C. (1997). Planning significant and meaningful research in exercise science: Estimating sample size. *Research Quarterly for Exercise and Sport*, **68**, 33–43.

Thomas, J. R., & Nelson, J. K. (1996). *Research Methods in Physical Activity* (3rd edn). Champaign, IL: Human Kinetics.

Thomas, J. R., Salazar, W. and Landers, D. M. (1991). What is missing in $p < .05$? Effect size. *Research Quarterly for Exercise and Sport*, **62**, 344–348.

Vincent, W. J. (1999). *Statistics in Kinesiology* (2nd edn). Champaign, IL: Human Kinetics.

Zhu, W. (1996). Should total scores from a rating scale be used directly? *Research Quarterly for Exercise and Sport*, **67**, 363–372.

Index